AWESOME
GOOD CLEAN
Jokes For Kids

BOB PHILLIPS

HARVEST
HOUSE
PUBLISHERS
Eugene, Oregon 97402

MORE AWESOME GOOD CLEAN JOKES FOR KIDS

Copyright © 1995 by Harvest House Publishers
Eugene, Oregon 97402

Phillips, Bob, 1940-
   More awesome good clean jokes for kids / Bob Phillips.
      p. cm.
   ISBN 1-56507-270-7
   1. Wit and humor, Juvenile.   I. Title.
PN6163.P485   1994
818′.5402—dc20   94-29224
                                              CIP
                                              AC

Printed in the United States of America.

About the Author

BOB PHILLIPS... is the author of over 30 books with combined sales of over 3,000,000 copies in print. He is a licensed marriage, family, and child counselor in California. Bob received his bachelor's degree from Biola University, master's degree from Cal State University in Fresno, and his Ph.D. in counseling from Trinity Seminary. He is presently the Executive Director of Hume Lake Christian Camps, one of America's largest youth and adult camping programs.

Contents

1

Funny Business

"Is she Hungary?" Wilbur asked.

"Alaska," said Wesley.

"Yes, Siam," she replied.

"All right. I'll Fiji," Wilbur offered.

"Oh, don't Russia," Wesley admonished.

"What if she Wales?" Wilbur demanded.

"Give her a Canada Chile," Wesley suggested.

"I'd rather have Turkey," she said. "Except that I can't have any Greece."

When the waiter brought the check, Wilbur asked Wesley, "Look and see how much Egypt you."

— & —

A lady purchased a postage stamp at the post office. "Must I stick it on myself?" she asked.

"No, madam," replied the postal clerk. "It would be better if you stuck it on the envelope."

— & —

Three boys were talking.

"I have my father's nose and my mother's eyes," said the first boy.

"I have my grandfather's forehead and my uncle's ears," said the second boy.

"I have my brother's pants," piped up the third.

— & —

A man called on the director of a television show. He was carrying a sledgehammer, a huge rock, and a large paper sack.

"In my act, I put this rock on my head, and my assistant breaks it with this sledgehammer. I take a bow and then walk off the stage."

"Well, what do you have in the paper sack?" asked the director.

"Aspirin," the man said.

— & —

Q: If you had a box of candles and matches, how would you make it weigh less?

A: *Take one out and it will be a candle lighter.*

— & —

Two leopards in the zoo had just finished lunch. One sat back against the bars and said, "Mm-mm-mm! That really hit the spots."

— & —

I just couldn't get good grades in masonry school. Studying was like banging my head against a brick wall.

— & —

A young man who just joined the army wrote his mother the following letter: "Dear Mom: For the last 21 years you have been trying to teach me to clean my room, hang up my clothes, eat good food, go to bed early, and shine my shoes. Well, the army has taught me to do the whole thing in one week. Love, Quentin."

— & —

Two kids were talking one day. The first boy said, "I have to get a calendar."

The other boy asked, "Why?"

The first boy answered, "Because yesterday I got sick so I wouldn't have to go to school, and then I found out it was Saturday."

— & —

The young couple couldn't wait to get married. They got the preacher out of bed at three in the morning to do the job.

The next day a headline in the paper announced, *Preacher Ties Knot In His Pajamas.*

— & —

Did you hear about the guy who put Band-Aids in the refrigerator? He wanted to have cold cuts.

—— & ——

The baby sardine was afraid of the submarine until his mother explained it was just a can full of people.

—— & ——

Two termites were going out for dinner.
"Let's go eat a house," said the first.
"No, let's eat a pagoda," said the second.
"No good," said the first. "You know how it is with Chinese food. You're hungry again an hour after you eat it."

—— & ——

Everybody knows about the man who ran over himself. No one would go to the store for him, so he ran over himself.

—— & ——

A man went to a psychiatrist insisting he had swallowed a horse. Nothing the doctor could say would convince him otherwise. Finally, the psychiatrist agreed to arrange an "operation."

At the hospital, the doctors put the man to sleep, then led a horse into the operating room. When the man awakened, he took one look at the animal and said, "That's not the one I swallowed. Mine was a black horse."

—— & ——

A grocer leaned over the counter and yelled at a boy who stood close to an apple barrel:

"Are you trying to steal those apples, boy?"

"No...no, sir," the boy faltered. "I'm trying not to."

2

Norbert & Nadine

Norbert: What's the difference between an elephant and a flea?

Nadine: I have no clue.

Norbert: An elephant can have fleas, but a flea can never have elephants.

— & —

Norbert: What asks no questions but receives lots of answers?

Nadine: I don't know.

Norbert: A telephone.

— & —

Norbert: What is the surest way to keep water from coming into your house?

Nadine: Beats me.

Norbert: Don't pay your water bill.

— & —

Norbert: What is the best name for the wife of a shoemaker?

Nadine: I can't guess.

Norbert: Peggy.

—— & ——

Norbert: What is the best name for the wife of an astronomer?

Nadine: I have no idea.

Norbert: Stella.

—— & ——

Norbert: What do you call a man who doesn't have all his fingers on one hand?

Nadine: You tell me.

Norbert: Perfectly normal, for his fingers are evenly divided between his two hands.

—— & ——

Norbert: What is a cheerleader's favorite drink?

Nadine: I give up.

Norbert: Root beer.

—— & ——

Norbert: What do you keep after giving it to some-one?

Nadine: Who knows?

Norbert: A promise.

—— & ——

Norbert: What is the difference between an old ten-dollar bill and a new one?

Nadine: You've got me.

Norbert: Nine dollars.

—— & ——

Norbert: What happens when you feed lemons to a cat?

Nadine: My mind is blank.

Norbert: You get a sour puss.

—— & ——

Norbert: What would you call a leopard that never takes a bath?

Nadine: It's unknown to me.

Norbert: The Stink Panther!

—— & ——

Norbert: What's black and white, white and black, and green?

Nadine: I'm blank.

Norbert: Two skunks fighting over a pickle.

—— & ——

Norbert: When did the pig give his girlfriend a box of candy?

Nadine: I'm in the dark.

Norbert: It was Valenswine's Day!

—— & ——

Norbert: What do you get when you cross a computer with an elephant?
Nadine: Search me.
Norbert: A computer with extra memory!

—— & ——

Norbert: What dog stands the best chance of winning the heavyweight title?
Nadine: You've got me guessing.
Norbert: A boxer, of course!

—— & ——

Norbert: What follows a cat wherever he goes?
Nadine: I pass.
Norbert: His tail.

—— & ——

Norbert: What cowboy hero fought crabgrass throughout the West?
Nadine: How should I know?
Norbert: The Lawn Ranger!

—— & ——

Norbert: What is Santa's favorite Easter candy?
Nadine: I don't know.
Norbert: Jollybeans!

—— & ——

Norbert: What is green and bumpy, and leaps over buildings in a single bound?

Nadine: I have no idea.

Norbert: Super Pickle!

3

Side Splitters

Q: If a goat should swallow a rabbit, what would be the result?

A: *A hare in the butter.*

— & —

I read in a newspaper about a kangaroo in the San Diego Zoo that has no pep. The vet diagnosed him as out of bounds.

— & —

Show me a guy who plays basketball in a tuxedo, and I'll show you a gym dandy.

— & —

Did you hear about the newlyweds who were so frail that they got knocked cold when their friends threw rice at them?

— & —

Q: In what way was Ruth very rude to Boaz?
A: *She pulled his ears and trod on his corn.*

— & —

I once prayed in a hotel and they charged me a 75-cent long distance charge.

— & —

We were losing one game 76 to 0, but we weren't worried. We hadn't had our turn at bat yet.

— & —

They asked my Uncle Ambrose if anybody in his family suffers from insanity. He said, "No, they all seem to be enjoying it."

— & —

Love makes the world go 'round, but laughter keeps us all from jumping off.

— & —

We had such a bad team that every time we took the field our manager got fined for littering.

— & —

I hate housework. You make the beds, you do the dishes, and six months later you have to start all over again.

— & —

Three little boys were bragging about how tough they were.

"I wear out a pair of shoes in a month," the first little boy said.

"I wear out a pair of jeans in a week," the second little boy said.

"That's nothing," the other little boy said. "I wear out a babysitter in 20 minutes."

—— & ——

Today's cars are aerodynamically designed.
They're built to sit in traffic jams at high speed.

—— & ——

The teacher in the school for pigeons had just about given up on one of her pupils. "Either you fly tomorrow, or I'll put a rope on you and tow you around," she said.

"Oh, don't do that," he said, "I don't want to be pigeon-toed."

4

The Answer Man

Q: Why did the boy sleep on the chandelier?
A: *Because he was a light sleeper.*

— & —

Q: Why did the man bring a rope to the baseball game?
A: *To tie up the score.*

— & —

Q: Why do you always insist on talking about the weather to your barber?
A: *You wouldn't have me talk about anything as exciting as politics to a man who is handling a razor, would you?*

— & —

Q: Why was the basketball player holding his nose?
A: *Someone was taking a foul shot.*

— & —

Q: Why did the baker quit making doughnuts?
A: *He was sick of the hole business!*

— & —

Q: Why can't a bicycle stand by itself?
A: *Because it's two tired.*

— & —

Q: Why did the boy take a ladder to the ball game?
A: *Because the Giants were playing.*

— & —

Q: Why did the hockey player color his teeth orange?
A: *So they'd be easier to find on the ice.*

— & —

Q: Why is a lie like a wig?
A: *Because it is a false hood.*

— & —

Q: Why is a pig in the house like a house afire?
A: *Because the sooner it is put out the better.*

— & —

Q: Why is Joe such a pain in the kitchen?
A: *He whips the cream, strains the soup, and makes the beef stew.*

— & —

Q: Why don't astronauts get hungry in space?
A: *Because they just had a launch.*

— & —

Q: Why are fishermen and shepherds not to be trusted?
A: *Because they live by hook and by crook.*

— & —

Q: Why does Santa Claus always go down the chimney?
A: *Because it soots him.*

— & —

Q: Why is a lawyer like a crow?
A: *Because he likes to have his cause heard.*

— & —

Q: Why does a preacher have an easier time than a doctor or a lawyer?
A: *Because it is easier to preach than to practice.*

— & —

Q: Why should we not believe one word that comes from Holland?
A: *Because Holland is such a low-lying country.*

— & —

Q: Why is a bride always unlucky on her wedding day?
A: *Because she does not marry the best man.*

5

How Now?

Q: How can you make a slow horse fast?
A: *Tie him up.*

— & —

Q: How do you make gold stew?
A: *Add 14 carrots.*

— & —

Q: How did the rocket lose its job?
A: *It got fired.*

— & —

Q: How can you tell a spring chicken?
A: *By the bounce in its step.*

— & —

Q: How do computers know what to eat?
A: *They read the menu!*

— & —

Q: How can you keep a fish from smelling?
A: *Stick a Band-Aid across his nose.*

— & —

Q: How did the Three Bears keep Goldilocks from reentering their house?
A: *They put a Goldi-lock on the door!*

— & —

Q: How does a pilot cook his meals?
A: *In a flying pan.*

— & —

Q: How many letters are there in the alphabet?
A: *Eleven...T-H-E A-L-P-H-A-B-E-T.*

— & —

Q: How does the weirdo feel about winter?
A: *It leaves him cold!*

— & —

Q: How do you spell cat backward?
A: *C-A-T B-A-C-K-W-A-R-D!*

— & —

Q: How do you make a turtle fast?
A: *Don't feed him.*

— & —

Q: How do you keep food on an empty stomach?
A: *Bolt it down.*

— & —

Q: How can you buy eggs and be sure they have no chickens in them?
A: *Buy duck eggs.*

6

Beatrice & Benedict

Beatrice: What did the balloon say to the pin?
Benedict: I have no clue.
Beatrice: Hello, buster.

— & —

Beatrice: What's a good pet for a conceited actor?
Benedict: I don't know.
Beatrice: A hamster!

— & —

Beatrice: What's big, purple, and lies across the sea from us?
Benedict: Beats me.
Beatrice: Grape Britain.

— & —

Beatrice: What do you call a male owl?
Benedict: I can't guess.
Beatrice: A wise guy.

— & —

Beatrice: What is big, likes peanuts, and has a trunk?
Benedict: I have no idea.
Beatrice: An oak tree with a squirrel in it.

— & —

Beatrice: What do you get when you cross a poodle and a cuckoo clock?
Benedict: You tell me.
Beatrice: A watch dog.

— & —

Beatrice: What were the highest mountains in the world before the Alps were discovered?
Benedict: I give up.
Beatrice: The Alps, of course.

— & —

Beatrice: What's another name for counterfeit money?
Benedict: Who knows?
Beatrice: Homemade bread.

— & —

Beatrice: What vegetable was known as "The King of Rock 'n' Roll"?
Benedict: You've got me.
Beatrice: Elvis Parsley!

— & —

Beatrice: What does a shark eat with peanut butter?
Benedict: My mind is blank.
Beatrice: Jellyfish.

— & —

Beatrice: What is the definition of impossible?
Benedict: That's a mystery.
Beatrice: Trying to pull a hair off a flea with boxing gloves on.

— & —

Beatrice: What do you get if you cross a ham and a karate expert?
Benedict: I don't have the foggiest.
Beatrice: Pork chops.

— & —

Beatrice: What is the difference between a girl and a horse?
Benedict: It's unknown to me.
Beatrice: I'll bet you have some swell dates.

— & —

Beatrice: What did the golf ball say to the golf club?
Benedict: I'm blank.
Beatrice: You drive me wild!

— & —

Beatrice: What's another name for a cowhand?
Benedict: I'm in the dark.
Beatrice: Hamburger helper!

— & —

Beatrice: What carries things but does not move?
Benedict: Search me.
Beatrice: A shelf.

— & —

Beatrice: What kind of dog would a chemistry professor have?
Benedict: You've got me guessing.
Beatrice: A laboratory retriever.

— & —

Beatrice: What is the best name for the wife of a marksman?
Benedict: I pass.
Beatrice: Amy.

— & —

Beatrice: What is the happiest state in the union?
Benedict: How should I know?
Beatrice: Merry land.

7

Crazy Thoughts

Anita: Herbie hides under the sofa and reports every time you're hugged?

Amy: Yes, he's a regular little press agent.

— & —

Little boy: Daddy, do you think clams are happy?

Father: Have you ever heard one complain?

— & —

Moose: I'd like a triple chocolate ice cream sundae with lots of nuts on top of the whipped cream.

Waiter: How about a cherry on top?

Moose: Golly, no! I'm on a diet.

— & —

Clayton: Where in the world are you going with that candy bag?

Conrad: I've got a 14-carat diamond ring in it, and I'm goin' to propose to my girl.

Clayton: Do you think she'll accept you?

Conrad: Sure—it's in the bag.

—— & ——

Joe: Are you crazy if you talk to yourself?

Moe: Only if you listen to yourself.

—— & ——

Rex: What is the opposite of sorrow?

Tex: Joy.

Rex: And the opposite of misery?

Tex: Happiness.

Rex: And what is the opposite of woe?

Tex: Giddyap!

—— & ——

Tyler: Did anyone laugh when you fell on the ice?

Travis: No, but the ice made a few cracks.

—— & ——

Zack: I'm exhausted! I was up until midnight doing homework!

Mack: What time did you start?

Zack: Eleven forty-five.

—— & ——

Nit: The surgeon removed a healthy appendix with a blunt scalpel.

Wit: What a pointless operation!

—— & ——

Mother: Sit down and tell me what your grades are in school.

Son: I can't. I just told Pop.

—— & ——

Prison warden: I've been in charge of this prison for ten years. Let's have a celebration. What kind of party do you suggest?

Prisoner: An open house!

—— & ——

Owen: I started life without a penny in my pocket.

Orin: So what? I started life without a pocket!

—— & ——

Mark: Which baseball team do you like best, the Red Sox or the Nylons?

Matt: The Red Sox.

Mark: But the Nylons get more runs!

—— & ——

Randy: I'd go to the ends of the earth for you.

Sandy: Yeah, but would you stay there?

—— & ——

Karl: Did they take an X-ray of your sister Sue's jaw at the hospital?

Kyle: They tried to, but the only thing they could get was a motion picture.

— & —

Corey: When I went fishing I saw a fish that weighed 20 pounds jump out of the water.

Carter: How do you know it weighed 20 pounds?

Corey: It had scales on its back.

— & —

Jonas: I've changed my mind.

Joshua: Well, it can't be any worse than your old one.

— & —

Gabriel: My father can hold up an auto with one hand.

Flora: He must be a very strong man!

Gabriel: Not particularly—he's a policeman!

— & —

She: Did you get hurt when you were on the football team?

He: No. It was while the team was on me.

— & —

Horace: Did you know that when there's lightning, cows hide in trees?

Harry: I never see them.

Horace: See how good they hide?

—— & ——

Reporter: Why did you go to the North Pole?

Adventurer: Because I wanted to feel on top of the world.

8

Who's There?

Knock, knock.
Who's there?
Vera.
Vera who?
Vera interesting.

— & —

Knock, knock.
Who's there?
Justin.
Justin who?
Justin time for dinner.

— & —

Knock, knock.
Who's there?
Albie.

Albie who?
Albie down to get you in a taxi, honey.

— & —

Knock, knock.
Who's there?
Arch.
Arch who?
Gesundheit!

— & —

Knock, knock.
Who's there?
Abe Lincoln.
Abe Lincoln who?
Don't you know who Abe Lincoln is?

— & —

Knock, knock.
Who's there?
Alex.
Alex who?
Alex in Wonderland!

— & —

Knock, knock.
Who's there?
Uriah.

Uriah who?
Keep Uriah on the ball.

—— & ——

Knock, knock.
Who's there?
Ice cream.
Ice cream who?
Ice cream 'cause I'm a cheerleader.

—— & ——

Knock, knock.
Who's there?
Zing.
Zing who?
Zing a song of blackbirds.

—— & ——

Knock, knock.
Who's there?
Gladys.
Gladys who?
Gladys summer.

—— & ——

Knock, knock.
Who's there?
Hugh.
Hugh who?
Hugh better watch out, you better not cry.

—— & ——

Knock, knock.
Who's there?
Isadore.
Isadore who?
Isadore locked?

9

Great Laughs

I am the center of gravity.
I am the capital of Vienna.
I am in every victory.
I am in valuable.
I can be seen in the midst of the river.
I could name three who are in love with me.
I have been in the grave.
I have been in heaven.
Still you look in vain to find me.
Who am I?
The letter V.

Q: A woman had seven children and half of them were boys. How could that be?
A: The other half were boys too.

Q: A nickel and a dime were crossing a bridge, and the nickel fell off. Why didn't the dime fall too?
A: Because it had more cents than the nickel.

—— & ——

A perfect example of minority rule is a baby in the house.

—— & ——

Two fathers were bragging about their children. "My daughter is brilliant," said the first father. "She was able to get her B.A. in only three years."

"That's nothing," said the other. "My daughter got a Ph.D. in only one year."

"That's impossible," said the first man. "How could she get a Ph.D. in one year?"

"She married him," his friend said.

—— & ——

Q: A farmer has 3 1/3 haystacks on the east side of his property. He also has 7 3/8 haystacks on the west side of his farm. When he puts all the haystacks together how many haystacks will he have?
A: One.

—— & ——

A man was just admitted to the hospital for surgery. He said to his doctor, "I'm so frightened. This is my first operation."

The doctor nodded his head and replied, "I know just how you feel, it's my first operation too!"

—— & ——

A small boy stood in the entrance to the cobbler's shop watching the man at work.

Boy: "What do you repair boots with, mister?" he suddenly asked.

Cobbler: "Hide," replied the cobbler sharply.

Boy: "E-r-r, eh?" asked the boy.

Cobbler: "I said hide," replied the cobbler sharply.

Boy: "E-r-r, eh?" asked the boy.

Cobbler: "I said hide," replied the cobbler impatiently.

Boy: "What for?" the boy insisted, somewhat surprised.

Cobbler: "Hide! The cow's outside," sighed the man.

Boy: "Don't care if it is. Who's afraid of a cow, anyway?"

—— & ——

Jamie: It must be kind of difficult to eat soup with a beard!

Warren: Yes, it's quite a strain!

—— & ——

Roses are red,
And your face is so pink;
Which proves you should speak
Only after you think.

—— & ——

A kangaroo was complaining to his psychiatrist: "I don't know what's the matter with me. I just don't feel jumpy anymore."

—— & ——

The movie I just saw shouldn't have been rated **PG**. It should have been rated **RR**—for rotten and ridiculous!

—— & ——

The next time you are discouraged and feeling sorta blue, take a look at the mighty oak, and see what a nut can do.

—— & ——

A young boy's parents had paid a visit to the home of a neighbor one evening. The neighbor thought, naturally, when she answered the doorbell the next morning and found the boy at the door, that his parents had forgotten something.

"Please, Mrs. Anderson," said the boy, "may I look at your dining room rug?"

The woman was surprised but said, "Why, of course, Jon-Mark. Come right in."

The lad gazed at the rug for several minutes. Then he turned to its owner: "It doesn't make me sick," he said.

—— & ——

Q: With which hand should you stir your cocoa?
A: *With either, but it is better to stir it with a spoon.*

— & —

Q: If a young boy should lose his knee, where would he go to get another?
A: *To a butcher shop, where kid-neys are sold.*

— & —

Teacher: Please name the four seasons.
Student: Duck season, rabbit season, deer season, and pheasant season.

— & —

Q: A duck was swimming in a pond, and a cat was sitting on its tail. How could that be?
A: *The cat was on the shore, sitting on its own tail.*

— & —

The teacher asked the class to draw a ring. But Ryan drew a square instead. "Why did you draw a square when I asked for a ring?" she said.
"It's a boxing ring."

— & —

Teacher: Please name the four seasons.
Student: Salt, pepper, garlic, and mustard.

— & —

There was only one piece of cake left on the plate, and Mama divided it between Barnaby and Lola. Barnaby looked at his mother's empty plate and said, "Mama, I can't enjoy my cake when you're not having any. Take Lola's."

10

Winston & Winifred

Winston: What is gray, has four legs, a tail, and a trunk?
Winifred: I have no clue.
Winston: A mouse going on a trip.

— & —

Winston: What bird can lift the heaviest weight?
Winifred: I don't know.
Winston: The crane.

— & —

Winston: What has blonde hair, a gorgeous dress, and a 30-pound stuffed turkey?
Winifred: Beats me.
Winston: Beauty and the Feast.

— & —

Winston: What is the least dangerous kind of robbery?

Winifred: I can't guess.

Winston: Safe robbery.

—— & ——

Winston: What do hippopotamuses have that no other animals have?

Winifred: I have no idea.

Winston: Baby hippopotamuses.

—— & ——

Winston: What's the difference between a cloud on a rainy day and a boy who is being spanked?

Winifred: You tell me.

Winston: One pours out rain and the other roars out with pain.

—— & ——

Winston: What do you call it when you eat three desserts?

Winifred: I give up.

Winston: Cutting back.

—— & ——

Winston: What's the difference between an orange and a yo-yo?

Winifred: Who knows?

Winston: You'd be a fine one to send out for oranges.

—— & ——

Winston: What has four legs, a curly tail, and an IQ of 200?

Winifred: You've got me.

Winston: Albert Einswine!

— & —

Winston: What barbarian conqueror was also a male model?

Winifred: My mind is blank.

Winston: Attila the Hunk!

— & —

Winston: What do you call it when the members of an orchestra go on welfare?

Winifred: That's a mystery.

Winston: Band-Aid.

— & —

Winston: What time is it when a pie is equally divided among four hungry boys?

Winifred: I don't have the foggiest.

Winston: A quarter to one.

— & —

Winston: What is the best name for the wife of a real-estate man?

Winifred: It's unknown to me.

Winston: Lottie.

— & —

Winston: What part of London is in France?
Winifred: I'm blank.
Winston: The letter N.

— & —

Winston: What are men's opinions of riding skirts?
Winifred: I'm in the dark.
Winston: They are divided.

— & —

Winston: What is appropriate material for an inventor to wear?
Winifred: Search me.
Winston: Patent leather.

— & —

Winston: What is the difference between a sewing machine and a kiss?
Winifred: You've got me guessing.
Winston: One sews seams nice, the other seems so nice.

11

Knee Slappers

Q: One day two fathers and two sons went fishing. Each caught a fish. But only three fish were caught. Why is that?

A: Because there were only three fishermen—a boy, his father, and his grandfather.

— & —

A father was trying to break up his daughter's habit of making too many telephone calls. In an effort to slow her down he made a small sign for the telephone, which read:

Is this call really necessary?

The next day he found this sign in its place:

How can I tell until after I have made it?

— & —

A toothless termite walked into a saloon.
"Is the bar tender here?" he asked.

— & —

One friend of mine was so stupid he had to take the IQ test twice to get it up to a whole number.

— & —

A song heard by a hive: "Bee it ever so humble, there's no place like comb."

— & —

During a Ping Pong game, one of the contestants accidentally swallowed the ball. The ambulance came and rushed him off to the hospital, where he was quickly rushed into the operating room.

When he recovered after the operation, he noticed a dozen scars all over his body, some on his chest, some on his stomach. "Why did you cut me in so many places?" he asked the doctor.

"That's the way the ball bounces," answered the surgeon.

— & —

Q: A man spent a week in the mountains. He left on Friday and came back on the same Friday. How did he do it?

A: *His donkey was named Friday.*

— & —

Did you hear about the woman who cooked so many TV dinners that she thought she was in show business?

—— & ——

I was a five-letter man my first year in college and the letters were F-L-U-N-K.

—— & ——

Football is getting rough. You have to wear shoulder pads, a face mask, and a helmet . . . and that's just to sit in the stands.

—— & ——

It's tough to go through an identity crisis when you're apathetic.

You don't know who you are, and you couldn't care less about finding the answer.

—— & ——

I won't say my house is a mess, but have you ever seen a fly land in a cloud of dust?

—— & ——

Q: If you woke up in the night, what would you do for a light?

A: *Take a feather from the pillow; that's light enough.*

—— & ——

On our team, we got very few hits. If anybody reached first base, he had to stop and ask for directions.

—— & ——

Q: A man came home without his key and found all the doors and windows locked. How did he get in?
A: He raced around the house until he was "all in."

—— & ——

I was on an airline that was so cheap, when they rolled those little steps away, the plane fell over on its side.

—— & ——

They say that marriage makes a man dizzy, and it's true. As soon as I got a wife, I lost my balance at the bank.

—— & ——

Editor to writer: "Your book is a first-grade novel. Unfortunately, most of our readers have gone beyond the first grade."

—— & ——

Crime is really bad in my old neighborhood. On Christmas, Santa Claus comes down the chimney wearing a red suit and a matching ski mask.

12

The Answer Man

Q: Why was the moron able to buy ice at half price?
A: Because it was melted.

— & —

Q: Why did the elephant wear green sneakers?
A: His blue ones were at the laundry.

— & —

Q: Why wouldn't mother let the doctor operate on father?
A: Because she didn't want anybody else to open her male.

— & —

Q: Why is the sea measured in knots?
A: They keep the ocean tied.

— & —

Q: Why do women not become bald as soon as men?
A: *Because they wear their hair longer.*

— & —

Q: Why is it so hard to make frogs cry?
A: *They're always hoppy.*

— & —

Q: Why does it take longer to run from second base to third base than it takes to run from first base to second base?
A: *Because there's a shortstop between second and third.*

— & —

Q: Why is a cat like a transcontinental highway?
A: *Because it's fur from one end to the other.*

— & —

Q: Why does your sense of touch suffer when you are ill?
A: *Because you don't feel well.*

— & —

Q: Why does a policeman have brass buttons on his coat?
A: *To button up his coat.*

— & —

Q: Why would a compliment from a chicken be an insult?
A: *Because it would be fowl language.*

— & —

Q: Why do lions eat raw meat?
A: *Because they don't know how to cook.*

— & —

Q: Why did the orange stop in the middle of the road?
A: *Because it ran out of juice.*

— & —

Q: Why did the silly kid put an alarm clock in his shoe?
A: *Because he didn't want his foot to fall asleep.*

— & —

Q: Why are dudes no longer imported into this country from England?
A: *Because a Yankee-doodle-doo.*

— & —

Q: Why do people laugh up their sleeves?
A: *Because that is where their funnybones are.*

— & —

Q: Why do Irish peasants wear capes?
A: *To "cape" them warm.*

— & —

Q: Why was the baseball player arrested in the middle of the game?
A: *He was caught stealing second base.*

13

Tell Me How

Q: How did the weirdo get rid of the dalmatian?
A: *He used spot remover!*

— & —

Q: How did Jonah feel when the whale swallowed him?
A: *Down in the mouth.*

— & —

Q: How would you speak of a tailor when you did not remember his name?
A: *As Mr. Sew-and-Sew.*

— & —

Q: How come you were born in Ireland?
A: *My mother wanted me near her.*

— & —

Q: How can you get into a locked cemetery at night?
A: Use a skeleton key.

—— & ——

Q: How can a baseball game end in a score of four to two without a man reaching first base?
A: The players are all women.

—— & ——

Q: How many soft-boiled eggs can you eat on an empty stomach?
A: Just one, after which your stomach wouldn't be empty.

—— & ——

Q: How can you row a boat all day and end up where you started?
A: Just keep the boat tied to the dock.

—— & ——

Q: How do you stop a 200-pound hamster from charging?
A: Take away its credit cards.

—— & ——

Q: How does a schizophrenic change a light bulb?
A: He asks one of his personalities to do it for him!

—— & ——

Q: How did the turtle keep three jumps ahead of the rabbit?
A: *He played checkers with him.*

—— & ——

Q: How do you know that robbers are strong?
A: *They hold up banks, don't they?*

14

Victor & Veronica

Victor: What is the most dangerous animal in the yard?
Veronica: I have no clue.
Victor: A clotheslion.

— & —

Victor: What is the best name for the wife of a gambler?
Veronica: I don't know.
Victor: Betty.

— & —

Victor: What suit lasts longer than you want it to?
Veronica: Beats me.
Victor: A lawsuit.

— & —

Victor: What would you say if I asked you out?

Veronica: I'd probably say nothing because I couldn't talk and gag at the same time.

— & —

Victor: What beverage represents the beginning of time?

Veronica: I have no idea.

Victor: Tea (T).

— & —

Victor: What pine has the longest and sharpest needles?

Veronica: You tell me.

Victor: A porcu-pine.

— & —

Victor: What would you get if you crossed a weirdo with a famous college football team?

Veronica: I give up.

Victor: Notre Dumb!

— & —

Victor: What do you call a golf ball after you hit it?

Veronica: Who knows?

Victor: Lost.

— & —

Victor: What is the best name for the wife of a doctor?
Veronica: You've got me.
Victor: Patience.

— & —

Victor: What beverage is appropriate for a prize-fighter?
Veronica: My mind is blank.
Victor: Punch.

— & —

Victor: What kind of jam cannot be eaten?
Veronica: That's a mystery.
Victor: A traffic jam.

— & —

Victor: What do people in Colorado call little gray cats?
Veronica: I don't have the foggiest.
Victor: Kittens.

— & —

Victor: What is appropriate material for a fisher-man to wear?
Veronica: It's unknown to me.
Victor: Net.

— & —

Victor: What is appropriate material for a filling-station operator to wear?

Veronica: I'm blank.

Victor: Oilcloth.

— & —

Victor: Which clothes last the longest?

Veronica: I'm in the dark.

Victor: Pajamas, for they are never worn out.

— & —

Victor: What has 50 heads but can't think?

Veronica: Search me.

Victor: A box of matches.

— & —

Victor: What three noblemen are mentioned in the Bible?

Veronica: You've got me guessing.

Victor: Barren fig tree, Lord how long, and Count thy blessings.

— & —

Victor: What is the sharpest tool mentioned in the Bible?

Veronica: I pass.

Victor: The Acts of the Apostles.

— & —

Victor: What has a head like a cat, feet like a cat, a tail like a cat, but isn't a cat?
Veronica: How should I know?
Victor: A kitten.

— & —

Victor: What did Adam first plant in the Garden of Eden?
Veronica: I don't know.
Victor: His foot.

15

More Craziness

First cowboy: He's a real tough hombre. Quick on the trigger too. His guns are blazing before they clear the holster.

Second cowboy: What's his name?

First cowboy: No-Toes Smith.

— & —

Judge: Why did you hit your dentist?

Man: Because he got on my nerves.

— & —

Girl: Would you love me just the same if my father lost all his money?

Boy: He hasn't lost it, has he?

Girl: No.

Boy: Of course, I would, you silly girl.

— & —

Barber: So you think I'm a good barber. Well, I suppose I inherited that.

Customer: Was your father a barber?

Barber: No. He was a famous orator.

—— & ——

Little boy (calling father at office): Hello, who is this?

Father (recognizing his son's voice): The smartest man in the world.

Little boy: Pardon me, I got the wrong number.

—— & ——

Ella: Would you rather have an elephant chase you or a lion?

Reginald: I would rather have the elephant chase the lion.

—— & ——

Norris: Well, how are you getting on in your new ten-room house?

Owen: Oh, not so badly. We furnished one of the bedrooms by collecting soap coupons.

Norris: Didn't you furnish the other nine rooms?

Owen: We can't. They're full of soap.

—— & ——

Mama Owl: I'm worried about Junior.

Papa Owl: What's the matter?

Mama Owl: He just doesn't give a hoot about anything.

—— & ——

Freshman: I went out for the football team today, and I think I made it.

Junior: What makes you think you made the team?

Freshman: Well, the coach took one look at me and said, "Oh, no, this is the end!"

—— & ——

Florence: I just can't find the man who'll make me the perfect husband.

Emily: Maybe you're asking too much.

Florence: Nonsense! All I'm looking for is a man who's kind and understanding. Is that too much to ask of a millionaire?

—— & ——

Motorist: How did you manage to eliminate the bad roads in this part of the country?

Farmer: Simple. When the going gets rugged, we don't call it a road; we call it a detour.

—— & ——

Geraldine: He was wonderful. Divine. He said things to me no man ever said.

Rhoda: What was that?

Geraldine: He asked me to marry him.

—— & ——

Football player: Coach, my doctor says I can't play football.

Coach: You didn't have to go to a doctor. I could have told you that.

—— & ——

Mother: What are you doing, Flora?

Little Flora: I'm writing a letter to my friend, Cindy.

Mother: But you don't know how to write.

Little Flora: That's okay! Cindy doesn't know how to read.

—— & ——

He (at the movies): Can you see all right?

She: Yes.

He: Is there a draft on you?

She: No.

He: Is your seat comfortable?

She: Yes.

He: Will you change places with me?

—— & ——

Man: I'm in a hurry. Will the pancakes be long?

Waiter: No, sir, they will be round.

—— & ——

Willard: Excuse me, I think you are sitting in my seat.

Tough guy: Yeah? Prove it.

Willard: I left my pie and ice cream on it.

—— & ——

Barber: Well, my little man, and how would you like your hair cut?

Small boy: If you please, sir, just like father's, and don't forget the little round hole at the top where the head comes through.

—— & ——

Reginald: You know, I used to go around with her until I found out she spent $5000 a year on dresses.

Duncan: So you broke up over that?

Reginald: Yeah. Now I'm going with her dressmaker.

—— & ——

Harry: My big brother shaves every day.

Larry: That's nothing! Mine shaves 50 times a day.

Harry: He must be crazy.

Larry: No, he's a barber.

—— & ——

Boy: Oh, darling, I love you so much. Please say you'll be mine. I'm not rich like Quinten Everrich. I haven't a car, or a fine house, or a well-stocked cellar, like Quinten Everrich, but darling, I love you. I cannot live without you.

Girl: And I love you, too, darling; but where is this guy Quinten Everrich?

—— & ——

Eskimo boy: I drove a dogsled across the Arctic just to see you.

Eskimo girl: Oh, that's a lot of mush.

16

Open the Door

Knock, knock.
Who's there?
Watson.
Watson who?
Nothing much, Watson new with you?

— & —

Knock, knock.
Who's there?
Marsha.
Marsha who?
Marshamallow.

— & —

Knock, knock.
Who's there?
Me.

Me who?
Don't you know your name?

— & —

Knock, knock.
Who's there?
Soda lady.
Soda lady who?
Quit yodeling and let me in!

— & —

Knock, knock.
Who's there?
Canoe.
Canoe who?
Canoe come out and play?

— & —

Knock, knock.
Who's there?
Doughnut.
Doughnut who?
Doughnut bother me with silly questions!

— & —

Knock, knock.
Who's there?
Carla.
Carla who?
Carla locksmith. My key won't work.

— & —

Knock, knock.
Who's there?
Ben.
Ben who?
Ben looking all over for you.

— & —

Knock, knock.
Who's there?
Aaron.
Aaron who?
Aaron out my stinky gym locker!

— & —

Knock, knock.
Who's there?
My panther.
My panther who?
My panther falling down.

— & —

Knock, knock.
Who's there?
Hank.
Hank who?
You're welcome!

— & —

Knock, knock.
Who's there?
Annette.
Annette who?
Annette is needed to catch butterflies.

—— & ——

Knock, knock.
Who's there?
Pasture.
Pasture who?
Pasture bedtime, isn't it?

—— & ——

Knock, knock.
Who's there?
Thistle.
Thistle who?
Thistle teach you a lesson not to ask silly questions.

17

School Daze

Teacher: There will be only a half day of school this morning.

Pupils: Whoopee! Hooray!

Teacher: We'll have the other half this afternoon.

— & —

Teacher: Frankie, give me a sentence with the word "Camelot" in it.

Student: Right, teacher. A camelot is a place where the Arabs park their camels!

— & —

"The principal thinks I am very responsible," the boy told his mother. "Every time something goes wrong at school, he says I am responsible."

— & —

Teacher: This is the fifth day this week you're late! What do you have to say for yourself?

Student: I'm sure glad it's Friday.

—— & ——

Teacher: If you had five pieces of candy, and Joey asked you for one, how many pieces would you have left?

Student: Five.

—— & ——

Student: I don't have a pencil to take this exam.

Teacher: What would you think of a soldier who went into battle without a gun?

Student: I'd think he was an officer.

—— & ——

Teacher: Name four animals that belong to the cat family.

Student: The mama cat, the papa cat, and two kittens.

—— & ——

A teacher sent this note home to the parents of one of her pupils: "Lester is trying—very."

—— & ——

Teacher: If you insist on talking, I'll have to send you to the principal's office.

Student: Oh, does the principal want somebody to talk to?

—— & ——

Principal: Are there any unusual children in your class?

Teacher: Yes, three of them have good manners.

—— & ——

Teacher: How would you treat a pig that's been stung by a bee?

Student: Apply oinkment.

—— & ——

Teacher: Birds, though small, are remarkable creatures. For example, what can a bird do that I can't do?

Student: Take a bath in a saucer.

—— & ——

Teacher: If I lay one egg on this chair and two on the table, how many will I have altogether?

Student: Personally, I don't believe you can do it.

—— & ——

Teacher: If you had three apples and ate one, how many would you have?

Student: Three.

Teacher: Three?

Student: Yes. Two outside and one inside.

—— & ——

Teacher: Did you reprimand your little boy for mimicking me?

Parent: Yes, I told him not to act like a fool.

—— & ——

Teacher: A job well done need not be done again.
Student: What about mowing the lawn?

—— & ——

Teacher: If I had ten oranges in one hand and six in the other, what would I have?
Student: Big hands.

—— & ——

Teacher: Tell me about the Iron Age.
Student: Sorry, I'm a little rusty on that subject.

—— & ——

Teacher: Does anyone have a garbage disposal unit in his home?
Student: Yes, ma'am, we have one, but it isn't in the house.
Teacher: Then where is it?
Student: Out in the pig pen.

—— & ——

Teacher: Name the four seasons.
Student: Football, basketball, baseball, and soccer.

18

Did You Hear?

Did you hear about the restless sleeper who bought a water bed? He tossed and turned so much that he made himself seasick.

—— & ——

Did you hear about the skunk who had no nose? He smelled terrible.

—— & ——

Did you ever hear the story of the new roof? It's over your head.

—— & ——

Did you hear the one about the cookie? It's crumby!

—— & ——

Did you hear the one about the electric eel? It's shocking!

— & —

Did you hear the one about the air conditioner? It's so cool!

— & —

Did you hear the one about the broken pencil? It's pointless!

— & —

Did you hear the one about the helium balloon? It's a gas!

— & —

Did you hear the one about the clouds? It's over your head!

— & —

Did you hear the one about amnesia? You'll probably forget it.

— & —

Did you hear the one about the Mississippi River? It's all wet!

— & —

Did you hear the one about the ruby? It's a real gem!

— & —

Did you hear the one about the electric drill? It's boring!

— & —

Did you hear the one about the Milky Way? It's out of this world!

— & —

Did you hear the one about the redwood? It's tree-mendous!

— & —

Did you hear the one about the owl? It's a hoot!

— & —

Did you hear the one about the snake? It's hiss-terical!

— & —

Did you hear the one about the dynamite? It's a blast!

— & —

Did you hear the one about the frog? It's toadly hilarious!

— & —

Did you hear the one about the tornado? It'll blow you away!

— & —

Did you hear about the compulsive golfer? He drove himself insane.

19

Silly Dillies

The Sunday school teacher was working with her primary group. "Do you know who Matthew was?" she asked.

When she received no answer she asked, "Do any of you know who Mark was?" Still no answer.

"I'm sure that somebody knows who Peter was," she said. "Can anyone tell me please, who was Peter?"

A little boy raised his hand and said, "I think he was a wabbit."

—— & ——

There was an umpire who was famous for wandering all over the baseball diamond. During one game, he got hit on the head by a foul ball and fell down.

The announcer said, "We've just witnessed the fall of the roamin' umpire."

—— & ——

Rumor has it that a boxer who gets beat up in a fight is usually a sore loser.

—— & ——

Roses are red;
Violets are blue;
I copied your paper,
And I flunked too.

—— & ——

Television programming is so bad these days that the best things on TV are the commercials.

—— & ——

A young man spoke to the father of his girlfriend. "Sir, your daughter has consented to become my wife."

"Well, don't blame me," her father said. "You should have known something like that would happen if you kept hanging around here five nights a week."

—— & ——

With a grinding of brakes the officer pulled up his car and shouted to a little boy playing in the field: "I say, sonny, have you seen an airplane come down anywhere near here?"

"No, sir!" replied the boy, trying to hide his slingshot. "I've only been shooting at that bottle on the fence."

—— & ——

Roses are red;
Roses are yellow;
Grandfather's teeth
Are lost in the Jell-O.

— & —

A farmer was driving his horse and buggy into town on a hot summer day. Suddenly the horse stopped in his tracks, turned to the farmer, and said, "Golly, it's hot, isn't it?"

The farmer was dumbstruck. He turned to his faithful old dog on the seat beside him and said, "Did you hear what I heard? That horse just talked."

"Yes," answered the dog, "but he's just like everyone else; he talks about the weather but won't do anything about it."

— & —

Two boys were spending the afternoon at the city zoo. "What would you do," one of them asked, "if you were the head keeper at the zoo and the monkeys got loose?"

"I'd get a monkey wrench," his friend said, "and tighten them up."

— & —

New husband: Somehow I don't think my wife knows her way around the kitchen.

His mother: What makes you say that?

New husband: Well, this morning I saw her trying to open an egg with a can opener.

— & —

Q: Is it safe to write a letter on an empty stomach?
A: *It is safe enough, but it is better to write the letter on paper.*

— & —

"Come, come, come," said one who was wide-awake to one who was fast asleep. "Get up, get up; don't you know it's the early bird that catches the worm?"

"Serves the worm right," said the grumbling sleeper. "Worms shouldn't get up before the birds do."

— & —

I wonder if you could say that when a dentist comes back from his vacation, it's back to the old grind.

— & —

The teacher did not like the way her pupils were continually looking at the wall clock in her class. Finally she put up a sign over the clock: "Time will pass, will you?"

— & —

A woman was visiting her husband in prison. She said, "Now don't worry about the million bucks you got in the holdup. I already spent it."

20

Wilbur & Wendy

Wilbur: What's red and white and blue all over?
Wendy: I don't know.
Wilbur: A candy cane holding its breath!

— & —

Wilbur: What do you get if you cross a rattlesnake with a doughnut?
Wendy: Beats me.
Wilbur: A snake that rattles and rolls.

— & —

Wilbur: What country do cows love to visit?
Wendy: I can't guess.
Wilbur: Moo Zealand!

— & —

Wilbur: What do you get if you cross a lizard with a baseball player?

Wendy: I have no idea.

Wilbur: An outfielder who catches flies on his tongue and eats them.

— & —

Wilbur: What would you get if you crossed a dog with a cartoon sailor?

Wendy: You tell me.

Wilbur: Pupeye!

— & —

Wilbur: What two letters of the alphabet do children like best?

Wendy: I give up.

Wilbur: C and Y.

— & —

Wilbur: What would you get if you crossed a radio commentator with a cheese?

Wendy: Who knows?

Wilbur: Rush Limburger!

— & —

Wilbur: What hand do you use to stir your coffee?

Wendy: My right.

Wilbur: I always use a spoon, myself.

— & —

Wilbur: What do you feed your pet frog?
Wendy: My mind is blank.
Wilbur: Croakers and milk!

— & —

Wilbur: What always has its eye open, but never sees anything?
Wendy: That's a mystery.
Wilbur: A needle.

— & —

Wilbur: What is an important aid for pet mice with bad breath.
Wendy: I don't have the foggiest.
Wilbur: Mousewash!

— & —

Wilbur: What's so fragile you can break it with a whisper?
Wendy: It's unknown to me.
Wilbur: A secret.

— & —

Wilbur: What's the difference between a dog and a hockey puck?
Wendy: I'm blank.
Wilbur: About two IQ points.

— & —

Wilbur: What can fill a whole house and still weigh less than a tiny mouse?
Wendy: I'm in the dark.
Wilbur: Smoke.

—— & ——

Wilbur: What is nothing but holes tied to holes, yet is as strong as steel?
Wendy: Search me.
Wilbur: A chain.

—— & ——

Wilbur: What did one pig say to another?
Wendy: You've got me guessing.
Wilbur: I'll give you lots of hogs and kisses.

—— & ——

Wilbur: What did the bull say to the cow?
Wendy: I pass.
Wilbur: When I fall in love, it will be for heifer.

—— & ——

Wilbur: What would you get if you crossed Prince Charles with Moby Dick?
Wendy: How should I know?
Wilbur: The Prince of Whales.

21

Swift Jokes

"My new car turned out to be a lemon," he said sourly.

— & —

"How time flies," he said weakly.

— & —

"I'll never go near another skunk again," he said distinctly.

— & —

"I went to Dodger Stadium and rooted for Atlanta," he said bravely.

— & —

"I never lie," he said horizontally.

— & —

"I see I can't pull the wool over your eyes," he said sheepishly.

— & —

"I love hotdogs," he said frankly.

— & —

"I'm not trying to pin you down," he said pointedly.

— & —

"Bow? Wow, wow!" he said doggedly.

— & —

"I didn't order the ham on white!" he said wryly.

— & —

"I use mouthwash every morning," he said breathlessly.

— & —

"I'm almost overcome with all that automobile pollution," he said exhaustedly.

— & —

"I use my camera when people aren't looking," he said candidly.

— & —

"You cut me to the quick," he said sharply.

— & —

"The lemonade needs more sugar," he complained bitterly.

— & —

"Let's go camping," he said intently.

— & —

"A crocodile sandwich, please, and make it snappy!"

22

Doctor, Doctor

Patient: Doctor, I'm terrified of robins. Every time I see one, I break into a cold sweat.

Psychiatrist: But why are you frightened of robins, Mr. Smith?

Patient: Aren't most worms?

—— & ——

Patient: Doctor, I feel like a trash can!

Doctor: Rubbish!

—— & ——

Patient: Doctor, I tend to get fat in certain places. What should I do?

Doctor: Keep away from those places.

—— & ——

Doctor: How were those pills I prescribed to improve your memory?

Patient: I forgot to take them!

—— & ——

Psychiatrist: Tell me, what is your biggest worry at this stage of your treatment?

Patient: It's thinking up a way to tell you I can't pay for today's session.

—— & ——

Patient: I want to thank you, doctor. The pain in my back is gone. What was it, rheumatism?

Doctor: No, your suspenders were twisted.

—— & ——

A man walked into a doctor's office with his suit ripped and his arms and face bleeding.

The nurse took one look at him and asked, "Have an accident?"

The man replied, "No thanks, I already had one."

—— & ——

Patient: Doctor, something is wrong with me. I keep thinking I'm a frog.

Doctor: How long has this been going on?

Patient: Since I was a tadpole.

—— & ——

Sick boy: Doctor, when I'm all better, will I be able to program a computer?

Doctor: Of course you will, young man.

Sick boy: That's funny. I couldn't program one before I got sick!

— & —

Lady: Doctor, doctor, my husband thinks he's an automobile.

Psychiatrist: Well, show him into my office.

Lady: I can't. He's double-parked outside.

— & —

The doctor told me my operation was fairly routine and not at all complicated. I told him to remember that when he makes out the bill.

— & —

Patient: Doctor, you've got to help me. My neck feels like a pipe and my muscles are as tight as steel bands.

Doctor: I think you should stop taking the iron pills.

— & —

Dentist: Stop making faces and waving your arms. I haven't touched your tooth yet.

Boy: I know. But you're standing on my foot.

— & —

Patient: I feel funny, doctor; what shall I do?

Doctor: Go on television as a comedian.

— & —

Patient: Doctor, every bone in my body aches.
Doctor: Just be grateful you're not a fish.

— & —

I think it's only fair that a doctor who prescribes a placebo should be paid with counterfeit money.

23

Ivan & Isabel

Ivan: What do you call a boomerang that doesn't come back?
Isabel: I have no clue.
Ivan: A stick.

— & —

Ivan: What is appropriate material for a dairyman to wear?
Isabel: I don't know.
Ivan: Cheesecloth.

— & —

Ivan: What is the best name for the wife of a civil engineer?
Isabel: Beats me.
Ivan: Bridget.

— & —

Ivan: Who was the strongest man in the Bible?
Isabel: I can't guess.
Ivan: Jonah; the whale couldn't keep him down.

—— & ——

Ivan: What beverage is appropriate for a golfer?
Isabel: I have no idea.
Ivan: Tea.

—— & ——

Ivan: What is always coming but never arrives?
Isabel: You tell me.
Ivan: Tomorrow.

—— & ——

Ivan: What letter is nine inches long?
Isabel: I give up.
Ivan: The letter Y; it is one-fourth of a yard.

—— & ——

Ivan: What did one arithmetic book say to the other?
Isabel: Who knows?
Ivan: I've got problems.

—— & ——

Ivan: What did one watch say to another?
Isabel: My mind is blank.
Ivan: Hour you doing?

—— & ——

Ivan: What did one shrub say to the other?
Isabel: That's a mystery.
Ivan: Boy, am I bushed.

— & —

Ivan: What is the difference between progress and Congress?
Isabel: I don't have the foggiest.
Ivan: Pro and con.

— & —

Ivan: What is the best name for the wife of a jeweler?
Isabel: It's unknown to me.
Ivan: Ruby.

— & —

Ivan: What time is it when you see a monkey scratching for fleas with his left hand?
Isabel: I'm blank.
Ivan: Five after one.

— & —

Ivan: What is the best name for the wife of a lawyer?
Isabel: I'm in the dark.
Ivan: Sue.

— & —

Ivan: What is a good way to kill time in the winter?
Isabel: Search me.
Ivan: Sleigh it.

— & —

Ivan: What is big enough to hold a pig and small enough to hold in your hands?

Isabel: I pass.

Ivan: A pen.

— & —

Ivan: What is the difference between a cat and a bullfrog?

Isabel: How should I know?

Ivan: The cat has nine lives, but the bullfrog croaks every night.

— & —

Ivan: What kind of servants are best for hotels?

Isabel: I don't know.

Ivan: The inn-experienced.

— & —

Ivan: What has four legs and flies?

Isabel: I have no idea.

Ivan: A horse.

24

Rib Ticklers

The other day I went to a flea market looking for a bargain. All I came home with was fleas.

— & —

A woman went to the store to buy some diapers for her baby. The clerk said, "That will be a dollar plus tax, ma'am."

"I don't use tacks. I use safety pins," the woman replied.

— & —

Q: If a telephone and a piece of paper should run a race, which would win?

A: *The telephone, because the paper would always remain stationery.*

— & —

Q: One morning a boy couldn't find his trousers. What did he do?

A: He raced around the room until he was breathing in short pants.

— & —

Have I got a neat neighbor. She's so neat she puts paper under the cuckoo clock.

— & —

The good news is my father just doubled my allowance. The bad news is two times zero is zero.

— & —

One day Jeremy's father brought his boss home for dinner. When Jeremy's mother served the meat, the little boy asked, "Is this mutton?"

His mother replied, "No. Why do you ask?"

"Because dad said he was going to bring home a muttonhead for dinner," Jeremy answered.

— & —

Q: A room with eight corners had a cat in each corner, seven cats before each cat, and a cat on every cat's tail. How many cats were in the room?

A: Eight.

— & —

I know I'm a lousy cook, but I never realized how bad until the other night when I caught the dog calling Chicken Delight.

— & —

Our house is such a mess, the termites tried to have us exterminated.

— & —

Q: If butter is 50¢ a pound in Los Angeles, what are windowpanes in New York?

A: Glass.

— & —

It is so simple to be smart. Just think of something stupid to say, then say the opposite.

— & —

Last Christmas, my father gave me a bat. First time I tried to play with it, it flew away.

— & —

According to an old superstitious belief, the wearing of a ruby would preserve one from injury by falling. A medieval king who wore a ruby ring asked his jester one day:

"What do you think would happen if I jumped off the highest part of the castle with this ruby ring on my finger?"

The jester replied with a ready wit worthy of his office, "The ruby, my lord, would probably not be hurt."

— & —

I know a guy who owes so much money to so many people, his answering machine just says, "Hi, your check's in the mail."

25

Belly Laughs

Roses are red;
Pansies are purple;
Drink too much pop
And you're liable to burple.

— & —

Once upon a time there was a bee race.
There were three entrants, a honey bee, a bumble bee, and a vitamin B. Naturally, the vitamin B won.

— & —

First hunter: Good heavens. Cannibals.
Second hunter: Now don't get in a stew.

— & —

One evening at the neighborhood miniature golf course a man and his wife found themselves following a young couple with a tiny baby. The couple had worked out a system. They would trade the baby back and forth between them after each shot. But progress was very slow.

Finally, the man and wife who were following them became impatient. The lady said, "It seems to me that you should have hired a babysitter."

"Oh," said the girl who was holding the baby at the moment, "we are the babysitters."

—— & ——

A courtship begins when a man whispers sweet nothings, and ends when he says nothing sweet.

—— & ——

First woman: Who is your favorite writer?
Second woman: My husband.
First woman: What does he write?
Second woman: Checks.

—— & ——

"Nathan," said his mother severely, "there were two pieces of cake in the pantry this morning, and now there is only one. How is that?"

"I don't know," replied Nathan regretfully. "It must have been so dark I didn't see the other piece."

—— & ——

Baseball players are getting too rich. They hit the ball now and have their chauffeurs run to first for them.

— & —

I once had a dog who really believed he was man's best friend.
He kept borrowing money from me.

— & —

Rumor has it that tall people live longer lives than short people.

— & —

Last week I asked my wife to make Hungarian stew for me, but she couldn't. She said the butcher shop was out of Hungarians.

— & —

They call it a family tree because if you look hard enough, you'll always find some nut or sap in it.

— & —

I know a guy who is always late for everything.
He was three years old at his first birthday party.

— & —

Karla had just hit her little brother. Her mother told her, "That was an unladylike thing to do. Ladies don't hit people. They outtalk them."

— & —

The first thing a boy learns who has received a chemistry set for Christmas is that he isn't ever going to be given another one.

26

Bertha & Bradley

Bertha: What should a fullback do when he gets a handoff?
Bradley: I have no clue.
Bertha: Go to a secondhand store.

Bertha: What do you get from a cow with a split personality?
Bradley: I don't know.
Bertha: Half and half!

Bertha: What would you get if you mixed a weirdo with a can of beans?
Bradley: Beats me.
Bertha: Dork and beans!

Bertha: What was sweet, yellow, and got creamed by Sitting Bull?

Bradley: I can't guess.

Bertha: George Armstrong Custard!

— & —

Bertha: What do you get if you cross a duck hunter with a parrot?

Bradley: I have no idea.

Bertha: A bird that says, "Polly wants a quacker."

— & —

Bertha: What do you get if you cross a pig and a cactus?

Bradley: You tell me.

Bertha: A porkerpine.

— & —

Bertha: What goes around the house peeking through cracks?

Bradley: I give up.

Bertha: The sun.

— & —

Bertha: What frontier lawman was famous for his indigestion?

Bradley: Who knows?

Bertha: Wyatt Burp!

— & —

Bertha: What do you call a daredevil flier who makes an emergency landing in the Grand Canyon?

Bradley: You've got me.

Bertha: Ace in the hole.

—— & ——

Bertha: What's yellow, fuzzy, and too tired to eat honey?

Bradley: My mind is blank.

Bertha: Winnie the Pooped!

—— & ——

Bertha: What did the man say when he drank some poison?

Bradley: I don't have the foggiest.

Bertha: This stuff just kills me!

—— & ——

Bertha: What do you call a player who falls asleep in the bullpen?

Bradley: It's unknown to me.

Bertha: A bulldozer.

—— & ——

Bertha: What do you get if you cross a pony with two dimes and a nickel?

Bradley: I'm blank.

Bertha: A quarterhorse.

—— & ——

Bertha: What did one eye say to the other?
Bradley: I'm in the dark.
Bertha: There's something between us that smells.

— & —

Bertha: What's the best way to get rid of a 100-pound worm?
Bradley: Search me.
Bertha: Invite a 1000-pound robin over for breakfast.

— & —

Bertha: What do they call someone who had the stew in the school cafeteria today?
Bradley: You've got me guessing.
Bertha: An ambulance.

— & —

Bertha: What do you get if you cross a cat with a cactus?
Bradley: I pass.
Bertha: An animal that gives you a pain whenever it rubs against your leg.

— & —

Bertha: What do you call a cookbook that gives recipes for using the yellow portion of eggs?
Bradley: How should I know?
Bertha: A yolk book.

— & —

Bertha: What dog loves to take bubble baths?
Bradley: I don't know.
Bertha: A shampoodle!

27

The Answer Man

Q: Why did the little hummingbird have to stay after school?
A: He didn't do his humwork.

Q: Why do farmers from Iowa build their pigsties between their houses and their barns?
A: For their pigs.

Q: Why did the exterminator examine his computer?
A: He heard there was a bug in the system

Q: Why do golfers bring an extra pair of pants with them when they play golf?
A: In case they get a hole in one.

— & —

Q: Why would a spider make a good ball player?
A: Because he is good at catching flies.

— & —

Q: Why do you call your dog "Fried Egg"?
A: Because he rolls over easy.

— & —

Q: Why is a river so rich?
A: It has two banks all its own.

— & —

Q: Why did the crow sit on the telephone pole?
A: He wanted to make a long distance caw.

— & —

Q: Why was the little shoe sad?
A: His father was a sneaker and his mother was a loafer.

— & —

Q: Why don't cannibals eat clowns?
A: Because they taste funny.

— & —

Q: What's a good way to keep your house warm?
A: *Put a coat of paint on it.*

—— & ——

Q: Why do firemen wear red suspenders?
A: *To hold up their pants.*

—— & ——

Q: Why did the farmer put corn in his shoes?
A: *To feed his pigeon toes.*

—— & ——

Q: Why does a dog dress warmer in summer than in winter?
A: *Because in the winter he wears a fur coat, while in summer he wears a coat and pants.*

—— & ——

Q: Why did the mouse run away from home?
A: *Because he found out that his father was a rat.*

—— & ——

Q: Why did the man bring a bag of feathers to the store?
A: *He wanted to make a down payment.*

—— & ——

Q: Why did the boy keep his bicycle in his bedroom?
A: *He was tired of walking in his sleep.*

—— & ——

Q: Why is it hard to remember the last tooth you had pulled?
A: *Because it went right out of your head.*

—— & ——

Q: Why does lightening shock people?
A: *Because it doesn't know how to conduct itself.*

28

When, When, When?

Q: When do chickens have eight feet?
A: *When there are four of them.*

— & —

Q: When is the toughest time to play horseshoes?
A: *When the shoes are still on the horses.*

— & —

Q: When is a black dog not a black dog?
A: *When he's a greyhound.*

— & —

Q: When a car dealer assures you your new car has something that will last a lifetime, what is he referring to?
A: *He is referring to the monthly payments.*

— & —

Q: When is a cow not a cow?
A: *When she is turned into a pasture.*

— & —

Q: When is an apple like a book?
A: *When it is red.*

— & —

Q: When is a clock at the head of the stairs dangerous?
A: *When it runs down and strikes one*

— & —

Q: When are you going to open your bakery?
A: *When I can raise the dough!*

— & —

Q: When is a duck 20 feet tall?
A: *When he's on stilts.*

— & —

Q: When is a yellow dog most likely to enter a house?
A: *When the door is open.*

— & —

Q: When a lady faints, what number will restore her?

A: *You must bring her two.*

29

Lots of Laughs

George: Grandma, if I were invited out to dinner, should I eat pie with a fork?

Grandma: Yes, indeed, George.

George: You haven't got a pie in the house that I could practice on, have you, Grandma?

— & —

Mother: What are you looking for, Calvin?

Calvin: I'm looking for a dime.

Mother: Where did you lose the dime?

Calvin: I didn't lose it. I just want one.

— & —

Baldheaded man: You ought to cut my hair cheaper, there's so little of it.

Barber: Oh, no. In your case we don't charge for cutting the hair, we charge for having to search for it.

— & —

Teacher: What would you do if a man-eating tiger were chasing you?

Student: Nothing. I'm a girl.

— & —

Mother: How did you come to fall in the lake?

Son: I didn't come to fall in. I came to fish.

— & —

Camper: Doctor, that ointment you gave me makes my arm smart.

Camp doctor: In that case, rub some on your head.

— & —

Tex: Do fish perspire?

Rex: Of course, what do you think makes the sea so salty?

— & —

Christy: Can I have 50¢ for a man who's crying outside?

Mom: What's he crying about?

Christy: Ice cream, only 50¢.

— & —

Wife: What should I serve with my meat loaf?

Husband: The antidote.

— & —

Mother: Dear, go and see how old Mrs. Smith is this morning.

Daughter (after returning): Mrs. Smith says it's none of your business how old she is.

—— & ——

Customer (in department store): Do these stairs take you to the third floor?

Saleslady: No, you have to walk.

—— & ——

Bus driver: What's the matter, sir?

Passenger: I can't stand going up hills. It makes me very nervous.

Bus driver: Then why don't you try what I do?

Passenger: What's that?

Bus driver: Close your eyes.

—— & ——

Orin: There is talk that the next war will be fought with television.

Owen: Well, I'm in training. I've faced some terrible programs.

—— & ——

"Where's the barber who worked the next chair?" asked the old customer as he was getting a shave.

"Hadn't you heard about Bill?" said the barber. "It was a very sad case. He grew nervous and despondent over poor business, and one day when a customer said he didn't care for a massage, Bill suddenly went out of his mind and slashed the customer's throat. He is in the asylum for the criminally insane now. Will you be having a massage, sir?"

— & —

Rex: When were you born?
Tex: April 2.
Rex: A day too late.

— & —

Clem: I have a rare old computer game that once belonged to George Washington.
Slim: But there were no computers back then!
Clem: That's what makes it so rare.

— & —

Bill: I dropped a glass on the floor and didn't spill a drop of milk.
Jill: Why is that?
Bill: It was a glass of water.

— & —

Farmer: What are you doing in my apple tree, young man?
Boy: Well, sir, the sign says, "Keep Off The Grass."

— & —

Dad: Is that young man serious about his intentions?

Daughter: He must be, dad. He asked me how much I make, what kind of meals we have, and how you and mother are to live with.

Larry: Do turkeys have good table manners?

Karry: No. They always gobble at the dinner table.

30

Jon-Mark & Malcolm

Jon-Mark: What do you call the time of prehistoric pigs?

Malcolm: I have no clue.

Jon-Mark: Jurassic Pork.

— & —

Jon-Mark: What do you use when a tree has a flat?

Malcolm: I don't know.

Jon-Mark: A lumberjack.

— & —

Jon-Mark: What goes boom, squash, boom, squash, boom, squash?

Malcolm: Beats me.

Jon-Mark: An elephant with wet sneakers.

— & —

Jon-Mark: What kind of bird always sounds cheerful?

Malcolm: I can't guess.

Jon-Mark: A hummingbird.

— & —

Jon-Mark: What did one queen bee say to the other queen bee?

Malcolm: I have no idea.

Jon-Mark: Mind your own bee's nest.

— & —

Jon-Mark: What kind of snack does a crazy millionaire resemble?

Malcolm: You tell me.

Jon-Mark: A dough-nut.

— & —

Jon-Mark: What kind of dog works at the United Nations?

Malcolm: I give up.

Jon-Mark: A diplomutt!

— & —

Jon-Mark: What is appropriate material for a fat man to wear?

Malcolm: Who knows?

Jon-Mark: Broadcloth.

— & —

Jon-Mark: What's pigskin used for mostly?
Malcolm: You've got me.
Jon-Mark: To hold pigs together.

— & —

Jon-Mark: What's an astronaut sandwich made of?
Malcolm: My mind is a blank.
Jon-Mark: Launch meat.

— & —

Jon-Mark: What do you get when you cross a dinosaur and a skunk?
Malcolm: That's a mystery.
Jon-Mark: A really big stinker.

— & —

Jon-Mark: What do you get when you cross a cat with a hyena?
Malcolm: I don't have the foggiest.
Jon-Mark: Gigglepuss.

— & —

Jon-Mark: What is the sound of a bee laughing its head off?
Malcolm: It's unknown to me.
Jon-Mark: Buzz. Buzz. Buzz. Plop.

— & —

Jon-Mark: What do you get if you cross an elephant with a spider?

Malcolm: I'm blank.

Jon-Mark: I don't know, but when it crawls on your ceiling, the roof collapses!

— & —

Jon-Mark: What do you call a cat that likes to dig in the sand?

Malcolm: I'm in the dark.

Jon-Mark: Sandy Claws!

— & —

Jon-Mark: What should a runner eat before a race?

Malcolm: Search me.

Jon-Mark: Ketchup.

— & —

Jon-Mark: What did the hummingbird say when it laid an ostrich egg?

Malcolm: You've got me guessing.

Jon-Mark: Ouch!

— & —

Jon-Mark: What is the hardest thing about learning to ride a bike?

Malcolm: How should I know?

Jon-Mark: The sidewalk.

— & —

Jon-Mark: What does the vegetable say when you tell it a joke?

Malcolm: I don't know.

Jon-Mark: Hoe-hoe-hoe!

— & —

Jon-Mark: What kind of dial should you not get too close to?

Malcolm: Beats me.

Jon-Mark: A crocodile.

31

Use the Doorbell

Knock, knock.
Who's there?
Sherwood.
Sherwood who?
Sherwood like to come in.

— & —

Knock, knock.
Who's there?
Isabel.
Isabel who?
Isabel busted?

— & —

Knock, knock.
Who's there?
Tank.

Tank who?
Tank you for coming to the door.

— & —

Knock, knock.
Who's there?
Kleenex.
Kleenex who?
Kleenex are prettier than dirty necks.

— & —

Knock, knock.
Who's there?
Despair.
Despair who?
Despair of shoes is too tight.

— & —

Knock, knock.
Who's there?
Harry.
Harry who?
Harry up, it's cold out here.

— & —

Knock, knock.
Who's there?
Hugh.
Hugh who?
Well, yoo-hoo to you, too!

— & —

Knock, knock.
Who's there?
Madeja.
Madeja who?
Madeja open the door!

—— & ——

Knock, knock.
Who's there?
Mark.
Mark who?
Mark the Herald Angels Sing!

—— & ——

Knock, knock.
Who's there?
Ben.
Ben who?
Ben walkin' the dog.

—— & ——

Knock, knock.
Who's there?
Howard.
Howard who?
Howard you like to be my Valentine?

—— & ——

Knock, knock.
Who's there?
Norma Lee.
Norma Lee who?
Norma Lee I don't ring other people's doorbells.

Knock, knock.
Who's there?
Phyllis.
Phyllis who?
Phyllis in on the news.

32

My, My, My

My doctor insulted my looks last week. He told me I had a weak heart and advised me to avoid severe shocks. His prescription was to break every mirror in my house.

— & —

My Uncle Newt is as strong as a horse. We just wish he had the IQ of one.

— & —

My grandfather always used to ask me, "What's more important, your money or your health?" I'd say, "My health." He'd say, "Great, can you lend me 20 bucks?"

— & —

My wife is so skinny, when she wears a fur coat she looks like a pipe cleaner.

— & —

My house is such a mess that the neighbors got a petition up against us. Now we all have to wipe our feet before going out.

— & —

My barber said, "Why don't you try something different for a change?" I said, "Okay, this time give me a good haircut."

— & —

"My teacher sure does like me," a little boy said one day when he came home from school. "I heard her tell another teacher that it was the happiest day of her life when I was promoted to the third grade."

— & —

"My father is certainly going to be surprised when I write to him," said the new graduate. "He always said I was so stupid that I couldn't even get a job. And in the last month I've had six."

— & —

My neck's as stiff as a pipe, my head's like a lump of lead and my nose is all stopped up. I don't need a doctor, I need a plumber.

— & —

My teenage daughter thinks freedom of speech gives her the right to make as many long-distance phone calls as she wants.

— & —

My wife went to cooking school and learned how to prepare food in ten greasy lessons.

— & —

My uncle died and left me 200 clocks, and I've been busy ever since winding up the estate.

— & —

My gym teacher said I could be a real muscle man if I wanted to be. He says I have the head for it.

— & —

My doctor told me this operation was absolutely necessary. I said, "For what?" He said, "To send my kids to college."

— & —

My wife's cooking is so bad, we have holes in our screen door where the flies go out.

— & —

My husband's cooking is so bad, I went into the kitchen once and saw a cockroach eating a Tums.

— & —

My psychiatrist found out I have two personalities, so he charged me twice as much. I paid him half and said, "Get the rest from the other guy."

— & —

My doctor is very conservative. If he doesn't need the money, he doesn't operate.

33

Daffy Dictionary

Q: If a letter gets dropped in a mud puddle what would it be?
A: *Blackmail.*

— & —

Q: What is an eye dropper called?
A: *A very, very careless person.*

— & —

Q: What is a flashlight?
A: *A case in which to carry dead batteries.*

— & —

Q: What is a forger?
A: *A person who is always ready to write a wrong.*

— & —

Q: What is jump?
A: *The last word in airplanes.*

— & —

Q: What is a mud pack?
A: *Self-putty.*

— & —

Q: What are parasols?
A: *Two men named Sol.*

— & —

Q: What is a bad driver?
A: *The guy you run into.*

34

Ryan & Rodney

Ryan: What do you call a rabbit with a lot of fleas?
Rodney: I have no clue.
Ryan: Bugs Bunny!

— *&* —

Ryan: What do you do with a blue whale?
Rodney: I don't know.
Ryan: Cheer him up.

— *&* —

Ryan: What ocean animals go to Hollywood?
Rodney: I can't guess.
Ryan: Starfish.

— *&* —

Ryan: What do you call an orange playing a trombone?
Rodney: I have no idea.
Ryan: A tutti frutti!

—— & ——

Ryan: What letters are most like a Roman emperor?
Rodney: You tell me.
Ryan: The C's are.

—— & ——

Ryan: What's the difference between TV and a newspaper?
Rodney: I give up.
Ryan: You can't wrap up the garbage in a TV set.

—— & ——

Ryan: What letters are invisible, but never out of sight?
Rodney: Who knows?
Ryan: I and S.

—— & ——

Ryan: What did the big rose say to the little rose?
Rodney: You've got me.
Ryan: Hiya, Bud.

—— & ——

Ryan: What is the difference between an oak tree and a tight shoe?

Rodney: My mind is blank.

Ryan: One makes acorns, the other makes corns ache.

— & —

Ryan: What is the best name for the wife of a gardener?

Rodney: That's a mystery.

Ryan: Flora.

— & —

Ryan: What is the best thing to put into a dish of ice cream?

Rodney: I don't have the foggiest.

Ryan: A spoon.

— & —

Ryan: What has two heads, one tail, four legs on one side, and two legs on the other?

Rodney: It's unknown to me.

Ryan: A horse with a lady riding sidesaddle.

— & —

Ryan: What driver does not need a license?

Rodney: I'm blank.

Ryan: A screwdriver.

— & —

Ryan: What kind of beans grow in a candy garden?
Rodney: I'm in the dark.
Ryan: Jellybeans.

—— & ——

Ryan: What is the price of the moon?
Rodney: Search me.
Ryan: Four quarters.

—— & ——

Ryan: What did the jack say to the car?
Rodney: You've got me guessing.
Ryan: Can I give you a lift?

—— & ——

Ryan: What is appropriate material for an artist to wear?
Rodney: How should I know?
Ryan: Canvas.

—— & ——

Ryan: What animal keeps the best time?
Rodney: I don't know.
Ryan: A watchdog.

—— & ——

Ryan: What's red and goes putt-putt?
Rodney: I have no idea.
Ryan: An outboard apple.

35

The Answer Man

Q: Why is the letter K like a pig's tail?
A: *Because it is the end of pork.*

— & —

Q: Why should men avoid the letter A?
A: *Because it makes men mean.*

— & —

Q: Why did the woman spray insect repellent on her computer?
A: *The program had a bug in it.*

— & —

Q: Why did you put a worm in your sister's bed?
A: *I couldn't find an iguana.*

— & —

Q: Why was the owl a poor student?
A: He just didn't give a hoot!

— & —

Q: Why does a man permit himself to be hen-pecked!
A: Because he's chicken-hearted.

— & —

Q: Why does a cow go over a hill?
A: Because she can't go under it.

— & —

Q: Why did the judge sentence the comedian to five years in jail?
A: He was involved in some funny business.

— & —

Q: Why is a horse like a lollipop?
A: Because the more you lick it the faster it goes.

— & —

Q: Why are football players cool?
A: Because they have a lot of fans.

— & —

Q: Why did the robber take a shower before holding up the bank?
A: He wanted to make sure he'd have a clean getaway.

— & —

Q: Why did the worm oversleep?
A: *Because he didn't want to be caught by the early bird.*

— & —

Q: Why did the dieter bring scissors to the dinner table?
A: *Because he wanted to cut calories.*

— & —

Q: Why are tomatoes the slowest fruit?
A: *They're always trying to ketchup.*

— & —

Q: Why did the boy jump in the mud and then cross the street twice?
A: *Because he was a dirty double crosser.*

— & —

Q: Why are cards like wolves?
A: *Because they belong to a pack.*

— & —

Q: Why did the football coach send in his second string?
A: *To tie up the game.*

— & —

Q: Why did the boy hold his report card over his head?
A: *He was trying to raise his grades.*

— & —

Q: Why is a tent like a baseball?
A: *Because they both have to be pitched.*

36

More Funny Business

Bertram: I have a real good radio. I can get Boston, Denver, and San Francisco on it.
Clyde: That's nothing. I can stick my head out the window and get chilly.

— & —

Jonas: I can lift a shark with one hand.
Bert: I don't believe you.
Jonas: Get me a shark with one hand, and I'll show you.

— & —

Wit: Have you ever tried to tickle a mule?
Nit: No, why should I?
Wit: You'd get a big kick out of it.

— & —

City man: Is your water supply healthy?
Farmer: Yes, we use well water.

— & —

Ted: Once there was a king. In front of him were three glasses. Two were full, one wasn't. Who was he?
Ned: Beats me.
Ted: Phillip the Third.

— & —

Dora: What's red and dingle-dangles?
Debby: I don't know.
Dora: A red dingle-dangle. What's green and dingle-dangles?
Debby: A green dingle-dangle?
Dora: No, they only come in red.

— & —

Horace: Did I ever tell you about the time I was face-to-face with a lion?
Harold: No. What happened?
Horace: There I stood without a gun. The lion moved closer and closer. He was growling. He was right on top of me.
Harold: Gosh! What did you do then?
Horace: I moved on to the next cage.

— & —

Cortney: I'm putting in a claim on my medical insurance for this bump on my head.

Cora: I see. You're hoping they'll settle for a lump sum, right?

— & —

Salesman: This new computer will do half of your company's work.

Boss: Good. I'll take two of them!

— & —

Mother: If you eat more cake, you'll burst.

Son: Well, pass the cake and get out of the way.

— & —

Lloyd: Have you ever seen a man-eating fish?

Lionel: Sure.

Lloyd: Where?

Lionel: In a seafood restaurant.

— & —

Albert: What is the best way to teach a girl to swim?

Andy: Well, you take her arm and gently let her down in the water, put your arm around her waist, and...

Albert: Cut it out. It's my sister.

Andy: Oh, push her off the dock.

— & —

First neighbor: How is your daughter getting along in her bookkeeping class at school?

Second neighbor: Terrific! Now, instead of asking for her allowance, she just bills us for it.

— & —

An airplane and a helicopter went fishing.

Airplane: I'll get the fishing poles. You get the bait.

Helicopter: Why do I have to get the bait?

Airplane: Everybody knows the whirlybird gets the worm.

— & —

Rex: Why did they put the acrobat in the sanatorium?

Tex: Because he flipped out.

— & —

Angry man: Little boy, have you seen who broke my window?

Little boy: No, but have you seen my soccer ball?

— & —

Husband: Honey, this lettuce tastes funny.

Wife: It shouldn't. It's clean. I even washed it with soap.

37

Where, Oh Where?

Q: Where were you born?
A: *I was only a little baby at the time. Do you remember where you were born?*

— & —

Q: Where did the boat go after it got sick?
A: *To the doc.*

— & —

Q: Where are walking sticks mentioned in the Bible?
A: *Where Eve presented Adam with a little Cain.*

— & —

Q: Where does King Kong plug in his computer?
A: *Anywhere he wants to!*

— & —

Q: Where did the witch of Endor live?
A: *At Endor.*

— & —

Q: If you are out of money, where can it always be found?
A: *In the dictionary.*

— & —

Q: Where is the headquarters of the Umpires' Association?
A: *The Umpire State Building.*

— & —

Q: Where did the farmer take his pigs on a sunny Sunday afternoon?
A: *On a pignic.*

— & —

Q: Where was the Declaration of Independence signed?
A: *On the bottom of the page.*

— & —

Q: Where is paper money mentioned in the Bible?
A: *Where the dove brought the green back to Noah.*

— & —

Q: Where did Noah keep his bees?
A: *In the ark hives.*

— & —

Q: Where do salmon go to sleep?
A: *On the river bed.*

— & —

Q: Where do fleas go in winter?
A: *Search me.*

38

Leftovers

Father: Congratulations! You talked on the phone for only 45 minutes instead of the usual two hours! What happened?

Daughter: Well, it was the wrong number.

Suzie: Mummy, why does it rain?

Mother: To make things grow. To give us apples, pears, corn, flowers—

Suzie: Then why does it rain on the pavement?

Kyle: I told my mirror a joke yesterday.

Nathan: What happened.

Kyle: It cracked up.

Customer: Are you supposed to tip the waiters around here?

Waiter: Well, yes, sir.

Customer: Then how about tipping me? I've been waiting for two hours.

—— & ——

Ted: Where does a 680-pound gorilla sleep?

Ned: Where?

Ted: Wherever he wants to!

—— & ——

Tex: Did you hear about the barn that turned to stone?

Rex: No, what happened?

Tex: The wind blew so hard it made the barn rock.

—— & ——

Mother: Were you a good little boy at kindergarten today?

Son: Yes, you can't get into much trouble standing in the corner all day.

—— & ——

Teacher: Give me a sentence using the word "politics."

Student: A parrot named Polly swallowed a watch, and now Polly ticks.

—— & ——

Junior: Dad, I can't find my baseball mitt.
Dad: Look in the car.
Junior: I did, but I couldn't find it.
Dad: Did you try the glove compartment?

—— & ——

Basketball player: We're going to win this game!
Basketball coach: I certainly hoop so.

—— & ——

Teacher: I wish you would stop whistling while you are studying.
Student: I'm not studying, just whistling.

—— & ——

Hotel clerk: Please wipe the mud off your shoes when you come into this establishment.
Clyde: What shoes?

—— & ——

Mack: I left my watch upstairs.
Jack: Don't worry—it will run down.

—— & ——

Teacher: What was your mother's name before she was married?
Student: I think it must have been Hilton. That's the name on our towels.

—— & ——

Billy: I make money with my drums.
Willy: Oh, you play with a band?
Billy: Nope, my pop gives me a dollar a week not to play them.

— & —

Red: My dog knows math.
Fred: Really?
Red: Yes, I ask him what 27 minus 27 is, and he says nothing.

— & —

Molly: My cat can say his own name.
Marcy: What is your cat's name?
Molly: Meow.

— & —

Little leaguer: Dad, what does a ballplayer do when his eyesight starts going bad?
Dad: He gets a job as an umpire.

— & —

Magican: I can turn a handkerchief into a bouquet of flowers.
Boy: That's nothing. I can go to the corner and turn into a drug store.

— & —

Moe: I'm going to sneeze.
Joe: At who?
Moe: At-choo!

— & —

Boy: Darling, I could die for your sake.
Girl: You are always saying that, but you never do it.

39

How About That?

Q: How does a Democrat define his political philosophy?
A: *I disagree with Republicans!*

— & —

Q: How many dinosaurs lived on vegetables?
A: *None. They all lived on the earth.*

— & —

Q: How did the cow feel when she couldn't give any milk?
A: *Like an udder failure!*

— & —

Q: How can you make 15 bushels of corn from one bushel of corn?
A: *Pop it.*

— & —

Q: How do we know that a dentist is unhappy at his work?

A: Because he always looks down in the mouth.

— & —

Q: How can you make a pearl out of a pear?

A: Add L to it.

— & —

Q: How did Adam and Eve feel when they left the Garden of Eden?

A: Put out.

— & —

Q: How can a man tell the naked truth?

A: By giving the bare facts.

— & —

Q: A man was locked in a room which had nothing in it except a piano. How did he get out?

A: He played the piano until he found the right key.

40

Signs of the Times

Sign in pet store:
Must Move—Lost our leash!

— & —

Sign in doctor's office:
An apple a day is bad for business

— & —

Sign in a garden:
Beware of vegetarians!

— & —

Sign on cement truck:
We dry harder.

— & —

Sign on birdhouse:
Home Tweet Home.

— & —

Sign in loan office window:
Come in and borrow enough to get out of debt.

— & —

Sign in TV ad in newspaper:
*Because of the president's speech
"The Invisible Man" will not be seen tonight.*

41

Tie Your Tongue in a Knot

Knott and Shott fought a duel. The result was that they changed conditions: Knott was shot, and Shott was not.

It was better to be Shott than Knott.

— & —

Jimmy Jack Hackett jilted Jill Brackett.

— & —

Rotten Roscoe rescued Rosie from the roaring rapids.

— & —

Rub rugs roughly.

— & —

Landlubbers love blubber.

— & —

Shameful sheep-sellers sell cheap sheep.

— & —

A swim well swum is a well-swum swim.

— & —

Three free-thinking frogs think friendly thoughts.

— & —

Trim these three fine free trees.

42

Lisa & Lila

Lisa: What do electricians study in school?
Lila: I have no clue.
Lisa: Current events!

— & —

Lisa: What's worse than finding half a worm in your apple?
Lila: I don't know.
Lisa: Finding a frog in your throat.

— & —

Lisa: What kind of teeth can you buy for a dollar?
Lila: Beats me.
Lisa: Buck teeth.

— & —

Lisa: What tree can you hold in your hand?
Lila: I have no idea.
Lisa: A palm.

—— & ——

Lisa: What has a beard and no legs?
Lila: You tell me.
Lisa: A chin.

—— & ——

Lisa: What kind of gum do bees make?
Lila: I give up.
Lisa: Bumble gum.

—— & ——

Lisa: What dessert is appropriate for a shoemaker?
Lila: Who knows?
Lisa: Cobbler.

—— & ——

Lisa: What is the best name for the wife of a train conductor in charge of the sleeping cars?
Lila: You've got me.
Lisa: Bertha.

—— & ——

Lisa: What letter is most useful to a deaf woman?
Lila: My mind is blank.
Lisa: The letter A, because it makes her hear.

—— & ——

Lisa: What is the best thing to take when one is run down?

Lila: That's a mystery.

Lisa: The license number of the car.

—— & ——

Lisa: What happens to a man who starts home to dinner and misses his train.

Lila: I'm blank.

Lisa: He catches it when he gets home.

—— & ——

Lisa: What is the main reason for using a cookie sheet?

Lila: I don't have the foggiest.

Lisa: For cookies to sleep on.

—— & ——

Lisa: What is the difference between a well-dressed man and a tired dog?

Lila: It's unknown to me.

Lisa: The man wears an entire suit, the dog just pants.

—— & ——

Lisa: What three letters make a man of a boy?

Lila: I'm in the dark.

Lisa: A-G-E.

—— & ——

Lisa: What kind of doctor would a duck become?
Lila: You've got me guessing.
Lisa: A quack doctor.

—— & ——

Lisa: What is the best name for the wife of a fisherman?
Lila: I pass.
Lisa: Nettie.

—— & ——

Lisa: What has 18 legs and catches flies?
Lila: I don't know.
Lisa: A baseball team.

—— & ——

Lisa: What is the difference between a new five-cent piece and an old-fashioned quarter?
Lila: I have no idea.
Lisa: Twenty cents.

43

(More)
Did You Hear?

Did you hear about the worm that joined the army?
He's in the apple corps.

— & —

Did you hear the one about the canyon? It's grand!

— & —

Did you hear the one about the soap cleaner? It's
real clean.

— & —

Did you hear the one about the toothache? It's a
pain!

— & —

Did you hear the one about the terrible twin boys? It's two bad!

—— & ——

Did you hear the one about the sewing machine? It'll leave you in stitches!

—— & ——

Did you hear about the dumb crook? He thought the easiest way to get some fast dough was to rob bakeries.

—— & ——

Did you hear about the patient with a split personality? He was so stuck up he wouldn't even speak to himself.

—— & ——

Did you hear the joke about the lunch meat? It's a lot of baloney.

—— & ——

Did you hear the joke about the bed? It hasn't been made up yet.

—— & ——

Did you hear the joke about the knife? It's a cut-up.

—— & ——

Did you hear the one about the boxer? It'll knock you out!

— & —

Did you hear the one about the rocket? It's out of sight.

— & —

Did you hear the one about the jungle? It's wild!

— & —

Did you hear about the train engine that went crazy? It was a loco-motive!

— & —

Did you ever hear the story about the two holes in the ground? Well, well.

— & —

Did you hear about the newlyweds who were so skinny that on their wedding day the guests didn't throw rice, they threw vitamins?

— & —

Did you hear the one about the salt mine? It's pretty deep!

44

Hoarse Laughs

Q: Who invented the first airplane that didn't fly?
A: Orville and Wilbur Wrong.

— & —

Q: Which is more valuable, a paper dollar or a silver dollar?
A: The paper dollar, because when you put it into your pocket you double it, and when you take it out you find it increases.

— & —

Q: Who was the first electrician in the Bible?
A: Noah; he made the ark light on Mount Ararat.

— & —

Q: Who's elderly, has many children, and walks around with sticky feet?
A: *The Old Woman Who Lives in the Glue.*

— & —

Q: Which NFL team would you not entrust with your valuables?
A: *The Pittsburgh Stealers!*

— & —

Q: Who performs operations at the fish hospital?
A: *The head sturgeon.*

— & —

Q: Which is heavier, a full moon or a half moon?
A: *A half moon, because a full moon is lighter.*

— & —

Q: Which has more legs, a cow or no cow?
A: *No cow; a cow has four legs, but no cow has eight legs.*

— & —

Q: Who writes nursery rhymes and squeezes oranges?
A: *Mother Juice.*

— & —

Q: Which is correct: The white of the eggs is yellow; or the white of the eggs are yellow?
A: *Neither. The whites are white.*

— & —

Q: Who had big ears, a trunk, and a size 27 glass slipper?
A: *Cinderelephant!*

—— & ——

Q: Who killed a fourth part of all the people in the world?
A: Cain, when he killed Abel.

—— & ——

Q: Which is the west side of a little boy's trousers?
A: *The side the son sets on.*

—— & ——

Q: Who's gloomy, writes mystery stories, and has a hangnail?
A: *Edgar Allan Toe.*

—— & ——

Q: Which is better, an old five-dollar bill or a new one?
A: *Any five-dollar bill is better than a one-dollar bill.*

—— & ——

Q: Who earns his living without doing a day's work?
A: *A night watchman.*

—— & ——

Q: Which state is round at both ends and high in the middle?

A: *O-hi-o.*

—— & ——

Q: Which is better: "The house burned down" or "the house burned up"?

A: *Neither, they are both very bad.*

45

Christy & Claudine

Christy: What do you call a deer who's a wimp?
Claudine: I have no clue.
Christy: A namby-pamby Bambi!

— & —

Christy: What did the beaver say to the tree?
Claudine: I don't know.
Christy: It's been nice gnawing you.

— & —

Christy: What would you get if you crossed a fuzzy yellow bear with a virus?
Claudine: Beats me.
Christy: Winnie the Flu!

— & —

Christy: What four letters of the alphabet would frighten a thief?
Claudine: I can't guess.
Christy: O I C U.

— & —

Christy: What's a tired tent called?
Claudine: I have no idea.
Christy: A sleepy teepee.

— & —

Christy: What goes "krab, krab"?
Claudine: I give up.
Christy: A dog barking backward.

— & —

Christy: What do you call two bikes that look exactly alike?
Claudine: Who knows?
Christy: Identical Schwinns.

— & —

Christy: What is everyone in the world doing now?
Claudine: You've got me.
Christy: Growing older.

— & —

Christy: What crime did the thief commit in the bakery?

Claudine: My mind is blank.

Christy: A pie-jacking!

— & —

Christy: What do you get if you cross a karate expert with a tree?

Claudine: That's a mystery.

Christy: Spruce Lee.

— & —

Christy: What is the difference between a crazy hare and a counterfeit coin?

Claudine: I'm blank.

Christy: One is a mad bunny, the other is bad money.

— & —

Christy: What kind of snake loves dessert?

Claudine: It's unknown to me.

Christy: A pie-thon, of course.

— & —

Christy: What is a duck's favorite TV program?

Claudine: I'm in the dark.

Christy: The feather forecast.

— & —

Christy: What do you call a hen that cracks jokes?
Claudine: Search me.
Christy: A comedi-hen.

— & —

Christy: What do you give a seasick elephant?
Claudine: You've got me guessing.
Christy: Plenty of room.

— & —

Christy: What is a frog's favorite drink?
Claudine: I pass.
Christy: Croaka-cola.

— & —

Christy: What's the difference between a gossip and a mirror?
Claudine: How should I know?
Christy: One speaks without reflecting and one reflects without speaking.

— & —

Christy: What do you call two spiders who just got married?
Claudine: I don't know.
Christy: Newlywebs.

— & —

Christy: What is the difference between a fisherman and a lazy schoolboy?

Claudine: I have no idea.

Christy: One baits his hook, the other hates his book.

46

Giggles

Barbie: I'm engaged to an Irishman.
Laurie: Oh, really?
Barbie: No, O'Reilly.

— & —

Mack: Are you a Giant fan?
Jack: Yes.
Mack: Well, I'm a little air conditioner.

— & —

Larry: I couldn't sleep last night.
Jerry: Why not?
Larry: I plugged the electric blanket into the toaster by mistake, and I kept popping out of bed all night.

— & —

Karl: Did you hear about the skunk who couldn't swim?

Eli: No, what about him?

Karl: He stank to the bottom of the pool.

— & —

Teacher: If you stood with your back to the north and faced due south, what would be on your left hand?

Student: Fingers.

— & —

Lady: Give me a ticket to Toledo.

Agent: Do you want to go by Buffalo?

Lady: No, I prefer to go by train.

— & —

Melody: I was in hot water last night.

Marcy: Why is that?

Melody: I had to take a bath.

— & —

Mother: I hear you've been fighting with one of those boys next door and have given him a black eye.

Son: Yes'm. You see, they's twins, and I wanted some way to tell them apart.

— & —

Mother: Son, the canary has disappeared.
Son: That's funny. It was there just when I cleaned the cage with the vacuum cleaner.

—— & ——

Mother: Auntie will never kiss you with a dirty face.
Son: That's what I thought.

—— & ——

Bill: I wish I had enough money to buy an elephant.
Jill: What in the world do you want an elephant for?
Bill: I don't. I just wish I had that much money.

—— & ——

Nit: What do you call a 200-pound man with a club?
Wit: Sir!

—— & ——

Boy: You need to learn more about baseball. Do you know what RBI stands for?
Girl: Really Boring Information.

—— & ——

Private: I've come to see General Parker.
Sergeant: I'm sorry, but the general is sick today.
Private: What made him sick?
Sergeant: Oh, things in general.

—— & ——

Rex: I went to see my girl last night.
Tex: Did you stay late?
Rex: Well, I guess I did, but I kept turning the clock back and finally my girl's father yelled down from upstairs and said: That clock has struck 12 three times now—would you mind letting it practice on one for a while?

— & —

Lydia: Where did he meet her?
Lucile: They met in a revolving door, and he's been going around with her ever since.

— & —

First sardine: How do you hug a hungry shark?
Second sardine: Very carefully.

— & —

Customer: When I bought this cat, you told me he was good for mice. He doesn't go near them.
Clerk: Well, isn't that good for mice?

— & —

Customer: I'd like some ginger ale, please.
Waiter: Pale?
Customer: No, just a glass will do.

— & —

Bill: What do you do?
Jill: I'm a dairy maid in a candy factory.
Bill: So what do you do?
Jill: I milk chocolates.

—— & ——

Mark: My father has Washington's shoe.
Clark: That's nothing. My father has Adam's apple.

47

Pure Silliness

Rustler: You mean you're gonna hang me?
Sheriff: Sure thing. On Monday morning.
Rustler: That's a terrible way to start the week.

—— & ——

Rex: Why did you become a printer?
Tex: I guess I'm just the right type.

—— & ——

Visitor: Do you like reciting, dear?
Child: Oh, no, I hate it, really. But mummy makes me do it when she wants people to go.

—— & ——

Moe: I wonder where your friend is.
Joe: Perhaps he overslept.
Moe: You know they kick everybody out of the park at eight in the morning.

—— & ——

Nathan: Haven't you ever met a girl you cared for?
Noble: Only recently. It was love at first sight.
Nathan: Why don't you marry her?
Noble: I took a second look.

— & —

Fox: Say, Beaver, they tell me you can cut down any size tree.
Beaver: Well, I've never been stumped yet.

— & —

Teacher: If I had two sandwiches and you had two sandwiches, what would we have?
Student: Lunch.

— & —

Q: Did Adam and Eve ever have a date?
A: No, they had an apple.

— & —

It's mostly you I care for. I care for your money only up to a certain point—the decimal point.

— & —

Orville: If two wrongs don't make a right, then what do two rights make?
Wilbur: An airplane.

— & —

Dad: If you're good, I'll give you a shiny new penny.
Lad: How about a dirty old nickel?

—— & ——

Customer: Would you mind taking the fly out of my soup?
Waiter: Do it yourself. I'm no lifeguard.

—— & ——

Slim: Say, did you know that most car accidents occur within ten miles of your house?
Clem: In that case, I'm moving to a new neighborhood.

—— & ——

Erika: Your pants look sad today!
Evan: Well, they're depressed!

—— & ——

Bill: What's the difference between a bumblebee and a mattababy?
Jill: What's a mattababy?
Bill: Why, nothing. What's the matter with you?

—— & ——

Dora: In the summer I get up as soon as the first ray of sun comes in my window.
Flora: Isn't that a bit early?
Dora: No, my window faces west.

—— & ——

Animal lover: What do turtles eat?
Animal expert: Bugs.
Animal lover: What kind of bugs?
Animal expert: Slow ones.

— & —

She: Tell me the story of the girl who bleached her hair.
He: I never tell girls off-color stories.

48

Lionel & Luther

Lionel: What dessert is always served in heaven?
Luther: I have no clue.
Lionel: Angel food cake!

— & —

Lionel: What do you call a meat thief?
Luther: I don't know.
Lionel: A hamburglar.

— & —

Lionel: What happened when the boy gorilla was
dumped by his girlfriend?
Luther: I can't guess.
Lionel: He went ape!

— & —

Lionel: What would you call a dinosaur who's a lousy driver?
Luther: I have no idea.
Lionel: Tyrannosaurus Wrecks!

— & —

Lionel: What is a cheerleader's favorite color?
Luther: You tell me.
Lionel: Yeller.

— & —

Lionel: What did the lunatic say to his girlfriend?
Luther: I give up.
Lionel: I'm crazy about you.

— & —

Lionel: What did the walls say to the floor?
Luther: Who knows?
Lionel: I have you surrounded.

— & —

Lionel: What do you call a happy Lassie?
Luther: You've got me.
Lionel: A jolly collie!

— & —

Lionel: Ask a question that cannot be answered with yes.
Luther: My mind is blank.
Lionel: Are you asleep?

— & —

Lionel: What is the best name for the wife of an upholsterer?
Luther: That's a mystery.
Lionel: Sophie.

— & —

Lionel: What kind of food improves your vision?
Luther: I don't have the foggiest.
Lionel: See-food!

— & —

Lionel: What did the dog say when he sat on sandpaper?
Luther: It's unknown to me.
Lionel: Ruff! Ruff!

— & —

Lionel: What do you call a little turkey that looks in other people's windows?
Luther: I'm in the dark.
Lionel: A Peeping Tom.

— & —

Lionel: What famous starship captain has some odd habits?
Luther: Search me.
Lionel: Captain James T. Quirk!

— & —

Lionel: What's that you have there?
Luther: A clamp.
Lionel: Oh, so you're a vise guy.

— & —

Lionel: What do you call a nutty dog in Australia?
Luther: I pass.
Lionel: A dingo-ling!

— & —

Lionel: What's the best paper for making kites?
Luther: How should I know?
Lionel: Flypaper.

— & —

Lionel: What kind of seal does housework?
Luther: I don't know.
Lionel: The Good Housekeeping Seal.

— & —

Lionel: What's the difference between a jeweler and a jailer?
Luther: I have no idea.
Lionel: One sells watches, and one watches cells.

49

Odds & Ends

Mary: Do you make up these jokes yourself?
Larry: Yes, out of my head.
Mary: You must be.

— & —

Daughter: Aw, shucks, ma. Why do I have to wash my face again before dinner?
Mother: Because you've got a smudge on it, hon.
Daughter: Why can't I just powder over it like you do?

— & —

Bill: I'm not myself today.
Jill: Yeah, I've noticed the improvement.

— & —

Waitress: Would you like your coffee black?
Customer: What other colors do you have?

— & —

Big sister: What did you learn in school today?
Little brother: Algebra.
Big sister: Say something in algebra.
Little brother: Pi *r* squared.
Big sister: No, no! Pie are round, cornbread are square!

— & —

Husband: Where is yesterday's newspaper?
Wife: I wrapped the garbage in it.
Husband: Darn it! I wanted to see it.
Wife: There wasn't much to see—just some orange peels and coffee grounds.

— & —

Bert: Do you think anyone can predict the future with cards?
Curt: My mother can. She takes one look at my report and tells me what will happen when my father comes home.

— & —

Justin: Did you know that Daniel Boone's brothers were all famous doctors?
Julius: No.
Justin: Don't tell me you've never heard of the Boone Docs?

— & —

Edgar: A snake bit me.
Eldon: Put something on it.
Edgar: I can't—it slithered away.

— & —

Christy: See you later, alligator.
Bob: After awhile, Gomer Pyle.

— & —

Juliet: Romeo, Romeo, where art thou?
Romeo: Down here in the bushes—the trellis broke!

— & —

Q: Have you ever heard of a baby raised on elephant's milk?
A: Yes, a baby elephant.

— & —

Clint: Have you been to Cape Kennedy?
Flint: Yes, it's a blast!

— & —

Norris: If you had a choice, would you rather be in a collision or an explosion?
Boris: A collision.
Norris: Why?
Boris: Because in a collision, there you are. But in an explosion, where are you?

— & —

First sheep: Baa-a-a
Second sheep: Moo-o-o
First sheep: Moo-o-o? Why do you say Moo-o-o?
Second sheep: I'm learning a foreign language.

— & —

Overheard (a college gal to friend): Jerry and I are going to have a secret marriage. Jerry doesn't even know about it yet.

— & —

Arnold: Did you know that bowling is the quietest sport?
Burt: No—how can that be?
Arnold: You can hear a pin drop!

— & —

Orin: Know what I'm going to be when I graduate?
Owen: A senior citizen?

— & —

Edna: Don't you think they make a perfect couple?
Elsie: Yes, I do. He's a pill, and she's a headache.

— & —

Randy: I'm nobody's fool.
Florence: Well, maybe someone will adopt you.

— & —

First explorer: Look! Here's a lion's track!
Second explorer: Great! You find out where he went, and I'll find out where he came from.

— & —

First actress (behind the scenes): Did you hear the way the public wept during my death scene?
Second actress: Yes, it must have been because they realized that it was only acting!

Other Books by Bob Phillips

WORLD'S GREATEST COLLECTION OF
CLEAN JOKES

THE RETURN OF THE GOOD
CLEAN JOKES

THE WORLD'S GREATEST COLLECTION
OF HEAVENLY HUMOR

THE WORLD'S GREATEST COLLECTION OF
RIDDLES AND DAFFY DEFINITIONS

THE WORLD'S GREATEST COLLECTION OF
KNOCK, KNOCK JOKES AND
TONGUE TWISTERS

THE BEST OF THE GOOD CLEAN JOKES

WIT AND WISDOM

HUMOR IS TREMENDOUS

THE ALL-NEW CLEAN JOKE BOOK

GOOD CLEAN JOKES FOR KIDS

THE ENCYCLOPEDIA OF
GOOD CLEAN JOKES

ULTIMATE GOOD CLEAN JOKES
FOR KIDS

AWESOME GOOD CLEAN JOKES
FOR KIDS

MORE AWESOME GOOD CLEAN JOKES
FOR KIDS

WACKY GOOD CLEAN JOKES FOR KIDS

NUTTY GOOD CLEAN JOKES FOR KIDS

LOONY GOOD CLEAN JOKES FOR KIDS

CRAZY GOOD CLEAN JOKES FOR KIDS

GOOFY GOOD CLEAN JOKES FOR KIDS

BIBLE BRAINTEASERS

THE GREAT BIBLE CHALLENGE

THE AWESOME BOOK OF
BIBLE TRIVIA

HOW CAN I BE SURE?

ANGER IS A CHOICE

REDI-REFERENCE

REDI-REFERENCE DAILY
BIBLE READING PLAN

THE DELICATE ART OF DANCING
WITH PORCUPINES

GOD'S HAND OVER HUME

PRAISE IS A THREE-LETTERED
WORD—JOY

FRIENDSHIP, LOVE & LAUGHTER

PHILLIPS' BOOK OF GREAT QUOTES &
FUNNY SAYINGS

THE ALL-AMERICAN QUOTE BOOK

BIBLE OLYMPICS

BIG BOOK—THE BIBLE—QUESTIONS
AND ANSWERS

THE UNOFFICIAL LIBERAL JOKE BOOK

WHAT TO DO UNTIL THE
PSYCHIATRIST COMES

For information on how to purchase any of the above books, contact
your local bookstore or send a self-addressed stamped envelope to:
Family Services
P.O. Box 9363
Fresno, CA 93702